NEW GENDER MAINSTREAMING SERIES ON DEVELOPMENT ISSUES

Engendering Budgets

A Practitioners' Guide to Understanding and Implementing Gender-responsive Budgets

Debbie Budlender and **Guy Hewitt**

Commonwealth Secretariat

Gender Section
Commonwealth Secretariat
Marlborough House
Pall Mall, London SW1Y 5HX
United Kingdom
Tel: +44 (0) 20 7747 6284
Fax: +44 (0) 20 7930 1647
E-mail: gad@commonwealth.int
www.thecommonwealth.org/gender
www.gender-budgets.org

Published by the Commonwealth
Secretariat
Layout design: Wayzgoose
Cover design: Pen and Ink
Cover photo: International Labour
Organization/P. Lissac
Printed by Formara Ltd.

Copies of this publication can
be ordered direct from:
The Publications Manager
Communications and Public
Affairs Division
Commonwealth Secretariat
Marlborough House
Pall Mall, London SW1Y 5HX
United Kingdom
Tel: +44 (0)20 7747 6342
Fax: +44 (0)20 7839 9081
E-mail:
r.jones-parry@commonwealth.int

ISBN: 0-85092-735-8

Price: £10.99

Related publications by the Commonwealth Secretariat

How to do a Gender-sensitive Budget Analysis, 1998
Gender Mainstreaming in the Ministry of Finance, 1999
Gender Budgets Make Cents, 2002
Gender Budgets Make More Cents, 2002

Gender Management System Series

Gender Management System Handbook
Using Gender-Sensitive Indicators: A Reference Manual for
  Governments and Other Stakeholders
Gender Mainstreaming in Agriculture and Rural Development:
  A Reference Manual for Governments and Other Stakeholders
Gender Mainstreaming in Development Planning: A Reference
  Manual for Governments and Other Stakeholders
Gender Mainstreaming in Education: A Reference Manual for
  Governments and Other Stakeholders
Gender Mainstreaming in Finance: A Reference Manual for
  Governments and Other Stakeholders
Gender Mainstreaming in Information and Communications:
  A Reference Manual for Governments and Other Stakeholders
Gender Mainstreaming in Legal and Constitutional Affairs:
  A Reference Manual for Governments and Other Stakeholders
Gender Mainstreaming in the Public Service: A Reference Manual
  for Governments and Other Stakeholders
Gender Mainstreaming in Science and Technology: A Reference
  Manual for Governments and Other Stakeholders
Gender Mainstreaming in Trade and Industry: A Reference Manual
  for Governments and Other Stakeholders
Gender Mainstreaming in the Health Sector: Experiences in
  Commonwealth Countries
Gender Mainstreaming in HIV/AIDS: Taking a Multisectoral
  Approach
Gender Mainstreaming in the Multilateral Trading System
Gender Mainstreaming in Poverty Eradication and the Millennium
  Development Goals
Integrated Approaches to Eliminating Gender-based Violence
A Quick Guide to the Gender Management System
A Quick Guide to Using Gender-Sensitive Indicators
A Quick Guide to Gender Mainstreaming in Development Planning
A Quick Guide to Gender Mainstreaming in Education
A Quick Guide to Gender Mainstreaming in Finance
A Quick Guide to Gender Mainstreaming in Information and
  Communications
A Quick Guide to Gender Mainstreaming in the Public Service
A Quick Guide to Gender Mainstreaming in Trade and Industry

About the authors

Debbie Budlender is a specialist researcher for the Community Agency for Social Enquiry (CASE), Cape Town, South Africa. A founding member of the South African Women's Budget Initiative, she is the leading international adviser on gender-responsive budgets, having worked in Africa, Asia, the Caribbean, Europe and the Americas. She has also written extensively on this area.

Guy Hewitt is Senior Manager at the Caribbean Examinations Council (CXC) in Barbados. He was previously a Senior Programme Officer in the Gender Affairs Department at the Commonwealth Secretariat, where he advised Commonwealth governments on the implementation of gender-responsive budgets and also provided technical support to other intergovernmental organisations and developmental agencies.

Publication team

Co-ordinators: Guy Hewitt and Donna St. Hill
Editor: Tina Johnson
Production: Rupert Jones-Parry

Contents

Abbreviations

ADB	Asian Development Bank
AIDS	acquired immune deficiency syndrome
ANC	African National Congress
CBP	Children's Budget Project
CEDAW	Convention on the Elimination of All Forms of Discrimination against Women
CGA	country gender assessment
CPIA	country policy and institutional assessment
CSO	civil society organisation
CSVR	Centre for the Study of Violence and Reconciliation
DAWN	Development through Active Women Networking Foundation
DfID	Department for International Development, UK
DISHA	Development Initiatives for Social and Human Action
FOWODE	Forum for Women in Democracy
GAD	gender and development
GDI	gender-related development index
GEM	gender empowerment measure
GMS	gender management system
GNP	gross national product
GRB	gender-responsive budget
GTZ	German Technical Cooperation Agency
HIV	human immunodeficiency virus
IDASA	Institute for Democracy in South Africa
IDRC	International Development Research Centre
IDS	Institute of Development Studies
IFI	international financial institution
IPU	Inter-Parliamentary Union
IMF	International Monetary Fund
MDG	Millennium Development Goal
MKSS	Mazdoor Kisan Shakti Sangathan
MLA	member of legislative assembly
MP	member of parliament
MTEF	medium-term expenditure framework
NGO	non-governmental organisation
NWM	national women's machinery
OAG	Office of the Auditor-General
PER	public expenditure review
PFA	Platform for Action

PIP	public investment programme
PRSP	poverty reduction strategy paper
SAP	structural adjustment programme
Sida	Swedish International Development Cooperation Agency
TGNP	Tanzania Gender Networking Programme
UN	United Nations
UNDAW	United Nations Division for the Advancement of Women
UNDP	United Nations Development Programme
UNECE	United Nations Economic Commission for Europe
UNICEF	United Nations Children's Fund
UNIFEM	United Nations Development Fund for Women
VCT	voluntary counselling and testing
WBI	Women's Budget Initiative
WILPF	Women's International League for Peace and Freedom
ZWRCN	Zimbabwe Women's Resource Centre and Network

Foreword

Heads of Government in Harare in 1991 declared gender equality to be a fundamental principle of the Commonwealth, and this was reaffirmed in the 1995 Commonwealth Plan of Action on Gender and Development and its Update. The Commonwealth is also committed to economic development and poverty reduction. Gender-responsive budgets (GRBs) can help governments uphold their commitments in all these areas and assist them in monitoring the implementation and gender impacts of policies and programmes. In addition, GRBs improve governance through increasing accountability, participation and transparency.

The idea of GRBs developed from the recognition that macroeconomic policies can narrow or widen gender gaps in areas such as income, health, education and nutrition, and can make the living standards of different groups of women and men better or worse. The Commonwealth's impetus towards encouraging member countries to integrate gender concerns into economic policy dates back to its pioneering work on women and structural adjustment in the late 1980s.

The Commonwealth Secretariat first launched a Gender Budget Initiative in 1995 and piloted the work in several countries, including Barbados, Fiji, South Africa and Sri Lanka. Since then, it has worked to develop analytical tools and disseminate findings and recommendations from its experience. It is currently integrating GRB analysis into its gender mainstreaming programme assistance to all member countries. The organisation is also undertaking work in the related areas of the informal economy, trade policy, public expenditure management and mainstreaming gender into ministries of finance.

Commonwealth governments deserve much credit for their support of GRB initiatives, in particular finance and women's ministers who have provided leadership. At their meeting in September 2002, Commonwealth finance ministers, as part of a wider commitment to work towards gender equality in economic policy-making, "agreed to make substantial progress on implementing gender-responsive budgets within their respective budget setting processes". This was the first time that gender was

If you want to see which way a country is headed, look at the country's budget and how it allocates resources for women and children.
Pregs Govender MP, South Africa

included as a specific agenda item at a meeting of any group of finance ministers.

Civil society organisations (CSOs) have also played an important role, with many gender budget initiatives at the country level being initiated by them. By engaging these different actors, this programme exemplifies the call in the 2002 Commonwealth Heads of Government Coolum Communiqué for stronger links between Commonwealth governments and civil society.

I would like to express my particular gratitude to the authors, Debbie Budlender and Guy Hewitt, for their continuing contributions in this field. They were two of the prime movers behind the publication of the Secretariat's other recent titles on GRBs: *Gender Budgets Make Cents*, which provides a conceptual framework; and *Gender Budgets Make More Cents*, which offers country studies and examples of good practice. Guy Hewitt also coordinated the project with Donna St. Hill; our thanks go to both of them, as well as to the editor, Tina Johnson.

As the authors stress, this guide does not attempt to provide a blueprint for implementing a gender-responsive budget. This is not possible, since not only is every situation different, but also adaptation to local contexts is essential to build capacity and ensure relevance and sustainability. Rather, the publication aims to provide practitioners with the basic information they need to understand GRBs and to start initiatives based on their own local situations.

Engendering Budgets is part of the Commonwealth's contribution to the global goal of gender equality, and we hope that it will prove useful to those already involved in, or considering work on, gender-responsive budgets.

Nancy Spence
Director, Social Transformation Programmes Division
Commonwealth Secretariat

Introduction

The explosion of gender-responsive budgets in the last eight years has been phenomenal. In 1995, there were only a few countries and agencies involved in this area. Today, however, a variety of groups operating at various levels have implemented some form of gender budget work in over sixty countries. In addition, many development agencies either have a GRB programme or support work at the country level. Encouragingly, there has been particular interest in countries new to democracy.

Whether it is seen as: (a) increasing the responsiveness of fiscal policy to poverty and social need; (b) enhancing governance; (c) supporting gender mainstreaming; (d) encouraging civil society participation; or (e) strengthening the monitoring and evaluation of outcomes of government action, the methodology used in gender budget work can help improve the efficiency, economy and gender equity of development strategies. The developmental value of GRBs is widely recognised and has been endorsed in the Beijing + 5 Outcome Document, the Monterrey Consensus and, most recently, in the Communiqué of the 2002 Commonwealth Finance Ministers' Meeting.

One of the strong features of gender budget work has been the desire of practitioners to adapt the methodology to their specific situation, needs, interests and capabilities. Based on the recognition that each context is unique, this willingness to innovate is one of the crucial ways of building in-country capacity and ensuring local ownership. These are essential if the initiatives are to be both relevant to the needs of the society and sustained over time. This guide was therefore prepared with some apprehension. The worry stemmed from the desire to avoid implying that there is a single recipe or blueprint for implementing a gender budget exercise. Too often, development interventions are limited by the importation of 'models of best practice', often by well-intended development agencies or 'experts', into situations bearing little resemblance to those from which the models were taken.

At the same time, however, basic information about gender

budgets needs to be made available so that practitioners can understand some of the fundamentals and determine how best these can be adapted to their local context. There is still a limited number of people with the necessary skills or availability to support the growing need for gender budget work. This guide therefore attempts to fill a specific gap in the literature and to assemble in one document some of the background information that practitioners should have at their disposal to answer questions about how to design and implement a GRB.

The guide consists of four parts:

Part 1: Getting Started. This section provides background information on GRBs. It includes a definition, a description of what these initiatives entail, a list of countries where work has taken place to date and examples of the diversity of experiences. It also provides the different rationales for undertaking the exercises.

Part 2: Understanding the Context. This part of the guide provides information on what a government budget is and the 'when, how and who' of its creation and implementation. Contained in this section is information on the budget process, the different groups involved in its preparation and potential entry points for beginning gender budget work.

Part 3: Implementing a Gender-responsive Budget. This section addresses the practical issues involved in implementation. It includes discussion on assessing the situation on the ground, who could be involved and their potential roles, and issues affecting the sustainability of these initiatives. Case studies are also included, as well as suggestions on how to access resources.

Part 4: Applying the Analytical Framework. The final section looks at how the three-way categorisation developed in Australia and the five-step approach developed in South Africa are applied. Information is included on the data required to analyse the situation of men, women, boys and girls; on how to assess the gender-responsiveness of policies; and on how to determine budgetary outputs and outcomes.

We hope that this guide to understanding and implementing

gender-responsive budgets will be useful to practitioners working in this area. A variety of supplementary materials is available at *www.gender-budgets.org*.

1. Getting Started

What are Gender-responsive Budgets?

Defining the work

Gender-responsive budget initiatives provide a way of assessing the impact of government revenue and expenditure on women and men, girls and boys. These initiatives are known by a range of different names. For example, they have also been referred to as 'women's budgets', 'gender-sensitive budgets', 'gender budgets' and 'applied gender budget analysis'. This book uses the term gender-responsive budget to refer to all these initiatives.

GRBs can help to improve economic governance and financial management. They can provide feedback to government on whether it is meeting the needs of different groups of women and men, girls and boys. For those outside government, GRBs can be used to encourage transparency, accountability and participation. They should also provide data that can be used in advocacy. For those both inside and outside government, gender budget work provides information that allows for better decision-making on how policies and priorities should be revised – and the accompanying resources needed – to achieve the goal of gender equality.

GRBs are not about dividing government money 50–50 between men and boys on the one hand, and women and girls on the other. A simple 50–50 division may look equal, but it is often not equitable, or fair. Instead, GRBs look at the full government budget from a gender perspective to assess how it will address the different needs of women and men, girls and boys, and different groups of women and men, and of girls and boys. For example, in the area of health, male and female people will have similar needs in respect to influenza and malaria. But women will have greater needs than men in terms of reproductive health.

However, GRB initiatives do not seek to create separate budgets to address women's or gender concerns. Special allocations for women and gender are sometimes helpful in addressing specific needs, but they are of limited use if the rest of the budget continues to privilege some citizens above others.

... gender budget work provides information that allows for better decision-making on how policies and priorities should be revised – and the accompanying resources needed – to achieve the goal of gender equality.

GRBs are about ensuring that government budgets are allocated in an equitable way so that the most pressing needs of
individuals and groups are satisfied. They are about ensuring
that when resources are scarce, the available resources are used
to assist those who are least able to provide for themselves.

> ### Box 1: Government Budgets and Gender
>
> The budget reflects the values of a country – who it values,
> whose work it values and who it rewards ... and who and
> what and whose work it doesn't. Past [South African]
> budgets are clear reflections of the priorities of apartheid,
> capitalist and patriarchal South Africa. The budget is the
> most important economic policy instrument of government,
> and as such it can be a powerful tool in transforming our
> country to meet the needs of the poorest. Government
> budgets and policies are often assumed to affect everyone
> more or less equally: to serve the 'public interest' and the
> needs of the 'general person'. Until now the average
> citizen targeted [in South Africa] has been white, male,
> Afrikaans and middle class. Yet in South Africa the average
> citizen is actually black, poor and a woman.
>
> Gender-disaggregated data are needed to demystify the
> apparent neutrality and, more specifically, the gender
> neutrality of the budget. It will expose how tariffs,
> industrial relations, taxation, education, employment or
> industrial policy impact on women due to their different
> location in the family and in the economy. Who gets the
> jobs and what is the nature of the jobs that are created?
> Who gets the subsidies? Who gets the housing and what is
> the nature of the homes and communities which are being
> developed? What are the traditional policy assumptions in
> the budgets, for example, are women dependent and are
> men the breadwinners? The fact of the matter is that the
> same rules and procedures can often reinforce existing
> inequalities and work against the interest of women.
> *Source:* Govender, 1996

Figure 1: Countries where GRBs have been Implemented

Africa	Americas	Asia	Europe	Middle East	Pacific
Botswana	Barbados	Afghanistan	Austria	Israel	Australia
Egypt	Belize	Bangladesh	Croatia	Lebanon	Fiji
Kenya	Bolivia	India	France		Marshall
Malawi	Brazil	Indonesia	Germany		Islands
Mauritius	Canada	Malaysia	Ireland		Samoa
Morocco	Chile	Nepal	Italy		
Mozambique	Ecuador	Pakistan	The former		
Namibia	El Salvador	Philippines	Yugoslav		
Nigeria	Mexico	Republic	Republic of		
Rwanda	Peru	of Korea	Macedonia		
Senegal	St Kitts	Sri Lanka	Norway		
South Africa	and Nevis	Thailand	Russia		
Swaziland	United	Vietnam	Scotland		
Tanzania	States of		Serbia and		
Uganda	America		Montenegro		
Zambia			Spain		
Zimbabwe			Switzerland		
			United		
			Kingdom		

GRBs have their greatest potential impact if they are ongoing rather than one-off and if they are driven by local groups rather than donors.

The figure shows that, since 1995, there have been GRB initiatives in more than 60 countries. There is clearly great interest in this area of work. However, many of the country initiatives have been one-off exercises – sometimes only a workshop with no follow-up. In addition, much of the work is dependent on external assistance. GRBs have their greatest potential impact if they are ongoing, rather than one-off, and if they are driven by local groups rather than donors.

Country examples: Australia and South Africa

GRB initiatives vary considerably across countries. These variations have been influenced by:

- The social and political context;

- Whether the initiatives are coordinated by governments, legislators or civil society organisations (CSOs);

- The capacity of the institution implementing them; and

- Whether the initiatives focus on national or sub-national levels.

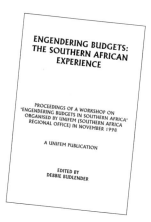

ENGENDERING BUDGETS:
THE SOUTHERN AFRICAN
EXPERIENCE

PROCEEDINGS OF A WORKSHOP ON
"ENGENDERING BUDGETS IN SOUTHERN AFRICA"
ORGANISED BY UNIFEM (SOUTHERN AFRICA
REGIONAL OFFICE) IN NOVEMBER 1998

A UNIFEM PUBLICATION

EDITED BY
DEBBIE BUDLENDER

Engendering Budgets: the Southern African Experience describes gender budget initiatives in Botswana, Mozambique, South Africa, Zambia and Zimbabwe.

The stories of GRB initiatives in Australia, South Africa and a range of other countries are told in Gender Budgets Make Cents *and* Gender Budgets Make More Cents.

Australia and South Africa are among the first countries to have had GRB initiatives. Their stories illustrate some of the ways in which initiatives can differ.

Australia

Australia was the first country to implement a GRB (called there women's budgets). The initiative started after the Labour Party gained power at the federal (national) level. Federal, state and territorial governments in the country assessed the impact of their budgets on women and girls over twelve years old between 1984 and 1996. Each government level developed a format that every government agency was required to use each year to audit its achievements in relation to women and girls. The initiatives covered all government expenditures, not just those directly related to women and girls. However, Australia did not specifically examine the situation of men and boys.

The South Australian women's budget divided expenditures into three categories, as follows:

1. *Women-specific expenditures:* allocations to programmes that specifically targeted groups of women and girls (e.g. aboriginal women's health initiatives and programmes to increase young women's access to non-traditional job training);

2. *Equal opportunities in the public service:* allocations to equal employment opportunities, such as programmes that promote the equal representation of women in management and decision-making, and equitable pay and conditions of service (e.g. training and mentoring programmes for women public servants and the review of job descriptions to remove gender bias);

3. *General or mainstream expenditures:* all the rest of the allocations that are not covered in the two categories above (e.g. identifying the users of legal aid and who accesses assistance to enter the export market). Although the analysis of this third category is challenging, these expenditures are the most important as they account for more that 99 per cent of government spending. Initiatives that overlook this category therefore ignore the most significant opportunities for promoting gender equality through public expenditure.

One challenge in doing the analysis is that governments often do not collect gender-disaggregated data on their services.

The women's policy offices (women's machinery) in Australia worked closely with treasury departments in coordinating and driving the women's budget initiatives. In most cases the report was published as one of the government's budget papers. The Australian initiative is thus a clear example of a bureaucracy-based strategy. The published results were presented to Australian women to communicate what the government had achieved in terms of its commitment to women's equality and women in development processes.

South Africa

South Africa has had two separate GRB initiatives – one involving non-governmental organisations (NGOs) and parliamentarians, and the other within the national government and led by the Finance Ministry. To date, the NGO-parliament initiative has been stronger and more sustained than the government one. The South African case is thus very different from that of Australia, despite drawing on some of its methods of analysis.

The NGO-parliament initiative, called the Women's Budget Initiative (WBI), began in mid-1995. That was the year after the end of apartheid, when the need to address past inequalities on the basis of race and gender, among other areas, was clear to everyone. The initiative was coordinated by two policy research NGOs and a parliamentary committee. However, it drew on a wide range of researchers and advisors situated in women's organisations, other NGOs, universities and government itself. Within the first three years, the initiative published three books that examined all 27 portfolios in the national budget. The books also included information on public sector employment, taxation and economic theory. Later analysis looked at donor funding to government, local government budgets, the impact of sectoral budgets on employment creation, non-tax revenue and a range of others issues.

To examine the different topics, the WBI uses a simple policy analysis approach involving five steps:

1. An analysis of the situation of women, men, girls and boys in a given sector;

2. An assessment of the extent to which sector policy addresses the (gendered) situation described in the first step;

3. An assessment as to whether budget allocations are adequate to implement the gender-responsive policy;

4. Monitoring of whether the money was spent as planned, what was delivered and to whom;

5. An assessment of whether the policy as implemented changed the situation described in the first step in the direction of greater gender equality.

The first two steps had been common in gender work before the WBI began. The third, fourth and fifth steps brought the added value of looking at budgets and resources.

In addition to the full analysis of each sector and topic, the WBI has published shorter, illustrated books that summarise the research in more simple language. The Initiative has also worked with a gender training network to produce workshop materials that allow the approach and information to be shared more widely.

The WBI sees the need for gender budget work both inside and outside government. It argues that government itself must have a GRB initiative in order to manage properly and be accountable. Government must use the initiative to monitor the gender impacts of its policies and budgets as well as to report on its activities to parliament and civil society. It must report in a systematic way that allows comparison of achievements and setbacks over the years.

An outside-government GRB initiative has a different purpose. It is about involving citizens in the important policy area of budgets, an area from which many people – particularly the marginalised and disadvantaged – have long been excluded. An outside-government initiative is about oversight and critique by parliament and civil society. It is about increasing available information so that advocacy for gender equality is strengthened.

Why Gender-responsive Budgets?

Gender-responsive budgets have caught the attention of gender and development advocates. Governments, civil society groups and multilateral and bilateral agencies are promoting their use as a central part of strategies to advance gender equality. This enthusiasm reflects the varied purposes GRBs can serve. These include, among others:

- Improving the allocation of resources to women;

- Supporting gender mainstreaming in macroeconomics;

- Strengthening civil society participation in economic policy-making;

- Enhancing the linkages between economic and social policy outcomes;

- Tracking public expenditure against gender and development policy commitments;

- Contributing to the attainment of the millennium development goals (MDGs) (Budlender et al., 2002:12).

Box 2: **Talking Points on Gender-responsive Budgets**

Why get involved in GRB initiatives?

- The budget is the most important policy of government because, without money, government cannot implement any other policy successfully.

- A GRB ensures that the needs and interests of individuals from different social groups are covered in the government budget. In particular, it ensures that the needs and interests of women, men, girls and boys are covered.

- Looking at budgets through a gender lens shows clearly where the collection and distribution of public money is unequal and inefficient. It also shows how discrimination affects national development.

Box 2 (continued)

- Budget analysis and advocacy by citizens brings together technical knowledge for effective and equitable policy-making with political and organising tools for engaging with powerful interests and institutions.

- Gender-responsive citizen budget initiatives complement anti-corruption strategies.

GRB initiatives ...

- do not propose separate budgets for women or for men;

- focus on gender awareness and mainstreaming in all areas of budgeting at all levels;

- promote the active participation of women stakeholders and other disadvantaged citizens who are excluded from public decision-making;

- promote more effective use of resources to achieve gender equity and transparency;

- look at the links between inefficient and inequitable use of resources based on gender and poor use of resources based on other axes of disadvantage such as race, ethnicity, geographic location and age;

- stress reprioritising within and across sectors rather than only an increase in overall government expenditure.

Benefits of GRB analysis for governments

- It can improve efficiency and impact by ensuring that expenditure benefits those who need it most.

- It can be used to report on progress on the government's commitment to democracy, equitable economic development, and women's rights and equality.

- It can be used to improve transparency and accountability and to help implement policies effectively.

Box 2 (*continued*)

- It can be used to track budgets and so reduce corruption.

- It provides a space for government to work with civil society to enhance development impact, democratic governance and transparency.

- It can be used to report on government's progress on compliance with national and international gender-related commitments, recommendations and action plans (e.g. national gender policies and the Convention on the Elimination of All Forms of Discrimination against Women (CEDAW)).

Benefits of gender-responsive analysis for women and citizen's groups

- It strengthens advocacy and monitoring initiatives by citizens.

- It provides information to challenge discrimination, inefficiency and corruption and to propose feasible policy alternatives.

- It recognises the ways in which women contribute to the society and economy with their unpaid labour in bearing, rearing and caring for citizens.

- It provides a way of holding public representatives accountable for their performance.

- It recognises the needs of the poorest and the powerless.

Adapted from unpublished training materials developed by Debbie Budlender and Lisa Veneklasen and used in workshops for the Asia Foundation.

Responding to gender disadvantage

During the last decade, a number of international meetings have been convened that have the potential for transforming the reality of women's lives. The World Conference on Human

*Gender equality is
... a fundamental
commitment
in the
Commonwealth.*

Box 3: Recognising the Need for Women's Economic Empowerment

In 2002, a new government gender-responsive initiative began in Gauteng Province, the second most populous province of South Africa and centre of the economy. At the province's Budget Lekgotla (retreat) of May 2002, it was agreed that departments needed to identify how their budgets could be engendered. Departments later came together for discussions and training on how this should be done. The approach is based on the new gender policy of the province, which draws on the Premier's identification of lack of access to economic empowerment as the core to women's inequality (fuelled by women's lack of education and skills).

The overview to the province's 2003/2004 budget statement notes that departments are encouraged to look at outcomes and outputs that: (a) specifically target women and girls; (b) benefit women or promote women's equality, although they may be used by both men and women; and (c) benefit women employees of the provincial government. Departments should also give a gender breakdown of their employees and provide targets in terms of procurement from women-owned businesses. The section notes that some departments have already done this, and that the government sees this process as an 'incremental' one aiming towards a 'fully fledged gender budget'.

Rights in Vienna (1993) asserted that women's rights are human rights. The International Conference on Population and Development (ICPD) in Cairo (1994) placed women's rights and health at the centre of population and development strategies. At the Fourth World Conference of Women in Beijing (1995), governments declared their determination "to advance the goals of equality, development and peace for all women everywhere in the interest of all humanity".

Gender equality is also a fundamental commitment in the Commonwealth. In 1995, it was embodied in a Common-wealth vision of a world "in which women and men have equal rights and opportunities in all stages of their lives" (1995 Commonwealth Plan of Action on Gender and Development).

However, declarations and policy commitments are not enough to put an end to the inequality that most women face. According to the most recent edition of *The World's Women*, the situation is still grim for many of them (United Nations, 2000):

- Nearly two-thirds of the illiterate people in the world are women;

- In developing countries, maternal mortality continues to be a leading cause of death for women of reproductive age;

- Women are still under-represented in decision-making in both government and business sectors, especially at senior levels; and

- Women's work continues to be very different in nature from men's. Women are engaged in less formal, lower status types of work and continue to receive less pay than men for the same work. Women also continue to do most of the unpaid work of bearing, rearing and caring for children and other citizens.

Engendering economic policy

Over the last decade there has been a growing recognition of the importance of macroeconomic policy in shaping women's living standards and their prospects for economic empowerment. In 1989, the Commonwealth and the United Nations Children's Fund (UNICEF) did pioneering work on the negative impacts on women of structural adjustment policies (SAPs). This work highlighted the need to integrate a gender perspective into macroeconomic policy.

Macroeconomics deals with economic models and financial aggregates. The critique of mainstream macroeconomics helped uncover the fact that while economic policy appears to be gender neutral (i.e. to have similar or identical impacts on men and women), it is in fact gender blind. The gender blindness comes about because policy-makers overlook the different socially determined roles, responsibilities and capabilities of women and men. As a result, the policy generally leaves

Over the last decade there has been a growing recognition of the importance of macroeconomic policy in shaping women's living standards and their prospects for economic empowerment.

... gender discrimination diminishes an economy's capacity to grow and to raise living standards.

women in an unequal position in relation to men, with less economic, social and political power.

There has also been a growing understanding of the ways in which gender inequality can constrain growth and other macroeconomic outcomes. The 2001 World Bank Report, *Engendering Development*, highlights the costs of gender inequality in terms of productivity, efficiency and economic progress. The Report notes that "by hindering the accumulation of human capital in the home and labour market, and by systematically excluding women or men from access to resources, public services, or productive activities, gender discrimination diminishes an economy's capacity to grow and to raise living standards" (p.11).

Box 4: **Gender Budget Work, SAPs and PRSPs**

The Ugandan and Tanzanian GRB initiatives were developed in response to the effects of structural adjustment programmes (SAPs) in these countries. In both countries, the NGOs that led the initiatives focused on education and health, which had suffered severe cutbacks in the first years of the SAPs.

Today, governments and external agencies in many countries are looking at ways of using GRBs in taking forward the poverty reduction strategy papers (PRSPs) that are the successors to SAPs. In countries such as Tanzania and Kenya, non-governmental groups have also tried to use the gender budget approach to influence and monitor the PRSP processes.

Diane Elson and Nilufer Cagatay (1999) suggest that there are three main reasons why macroeconomic analysis is usually gender blind:

1. *Economic institutions carry and transmit gender biases.* The institutions often ignore male biases in employment legislation, property rights and inheritance laws, all of which restrict and shape the economic activity of women.

2. *The cost of reproducing and maintaining the labour force is invisible because economic analysis does not consider unpaid work.*

Box 5: *The Different Value Given to Men's and Women's Educational Achievements*

In South Africa, as in many other countries, nurses and engineers provide a stark illustration of the different valuation of education leading up to work stereotypically female or male. In the early 1990s, nurses accounted for a quarter of all professional women and 96 per cent of all nurses were women. On the other hand, 96 per cent of all engineers were men. In 1992, a nurse who had completed a four-year degree at university earned a starting salary of 1,795 rand per month, while a student who had completed a four-year bachelors degree in engineering earned an average of 2,759 rand per month in the first year after qualifying. Moreover, an engineering technician with a qualification equivalent to completion of secondary school earned as much in the first year after study as a nurse with a four-year degree. Over the years, nurses have been required to do work of increasing complexity. Yet the real value of their salaries has fallen.

Source: Budlender, 1991

Women usually carry the main burden of looking after the household – cooking, cleaning and providing for family members, as well as ensuring community well-being. Although this unpaid care work is vital for maintaining the social fabric and reproducing the labour force, it is excluded in calculations of gross national product (GNP).

3. *Gender relations play an important role in the division of labour and the distribution of employment, income, wealth and productive inputs, all of which have important macroeconomic implications.* Particular occupations are often dominated by one gender. Regardless of education or skill level required, occupations dominated by women usually have lower earnings than those dominated by men (see box 5). In particular, women's skills such as nurturing, are given low value. For example, early childhood educators are paid less than mechanics, security guards and junior computer technicians, despite the importance of early childhood education for society.

Integrating the care sector[1]

Diane Elson has added the household and community care sector into a simplified macroeconomic model of national economic output (see Figure 2). The addition improves on the usual model taught in economics, which includes only the production of the private and public sectors. The relative size of the sectors varies depending on the level of development of a country and its economic and political strategy.

Figure 2: The Circular Flow of National Output – A Gender-aware Model

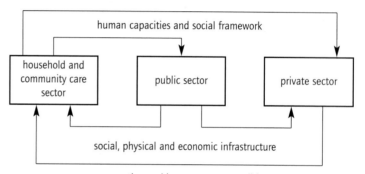

The three sectors shown in the model are interdependent. The private sector cannot create wealth for use by government, families and communities if the government, families and communities do not create wealth in the form of people and infrastructure for use by the private sector.

The private sector produces market-oriented goods and services for profit. The public sector produces social and physical infrastructure for use by the other sectors. It is market-oriented to the extent that its employees are paid wages and it is financed by government revenue. But it is less market-oriented than the private sector because it is not profit-oriented and delivers many services free.

The household and community sector produces goods and services as part of the process of caring for people. Work in this sector is not paid, although government may provide some support through child benefits, grants and subsidies. This sector

1 This section is based on Elson, 1997.

Woman carrying her infant while selling pineapples on the side of the road.

INTERNATIONAL LABOUR ORGANIZATION/
J. MAILLARD

is ruled by social norms rather than profit.

The fact that unpaid labour is missing in economic models means that it is often ignored in policy-making. For example, the costs of childcare in a public or private pre-school are included in the GNP and taken into consideration in policy decisions. But the costs of childcare done by mothers, older sisters, grandmothers and aunts are not included in the GNP and are usually not taken into account in policy decisions.

Box 6: **The Burden on Women of Reduced Health Spending**

Between 1983 and 1985, real spending on health fell by 16 per cent in Zambia. People had to travel greater distances, wait for longer periods of time to get treatment and drugs, and faced reductions in post-operative recovery. Women ended up spending more time caring for sick family members, including providing meals and helping to nurse them. This transfer of the costs of care to women had a knock-on effect as it placed additional burdens on women, often forcing them to be absent from paid employment.

Source: Elson, 2002b

... if the care sector is overburdened, it will harm the private and public sectors because they will be served by less healthy and productive human resources.

Most economists assume that women's time is available in unlimited quantities – that is, it has no cost to the individual, family and society. But if the care sector is overburdened, it will harm the private and public sectors because they will be served by less healthy and productive human resources. The care sector cannot be treated as a bottomless well from which water can always be drawn.

Addressing poverty and social need

In recent years, the processes of globalisation have accelerated. Some individuals, countries and corporations have gained. But many individuals, groups and countries have suffered. Overall, it seems that the gap between rich and poor countries, and between rich and poor groups within countries, has increased.

Government has a central role to play in addressing social need and promoting equity. In both developing and developed countries governments have recognised that GRBs can assist in: (a) poverty reduction efforts; (b) meeting the needs of vulnerable groups; and (c) promoting equity. Governments never have enough money to address all the needs and demands of citizens, corporations and others. By assessing the impact of different ways of spending its money, a government can allocate the available resources in a way that meets the most pressing needs.

Gender issues are important for understanding poverty and identifying strategies to reduce it. Women are less likely than men to be in paid employment. When employed, they are likely to earn less than men. They are more likely than men to work in the informal economy or in agriculture. But they have less access to finance, land and other resources to ensure decent earnings. Within poor households, women and girls often have less control over the available money and less access to household goods and public services than their male counterparts. They suffer violence on a large scale. They are more likely to be illiterate as well as politically and socially marginalised in their communities.

These gender differences determine the impact of government policies on women and men, girls and boys. For example, when Sri Lanka changed its food ration and subsidy programme in the 1980s, the real value of food stamps was reduced and the real incomes of poor households declined. Within poor

Box 7: Statistics on Poverty and Inequality

- The United Nations Development Programme (UNDP) reported in 2002 that the richest 5 per cent of the world's people had incomes 114 times the incomes of the poorest 5 per cent.

- The richest 1 per cent of the world's people receive as much income each year as the poorest 57 per cent.

- A total of 2.8 billion people in the world live on less than $2 a day.

- During the 1990s, the number of people in extreme poverty in sub-Saharan Africa increased from 242 million to 300 million.

- Today, 20 countries in sub-Saharan Africa are poorer than they were in 1990, and 23 are poorer than they were in 1975.

- The World Trade Organization allocates one vote per country. However, most of the important decisions are made by the leading economic powers in 'green room' meetings.

- Executive directors representing France, Germany, Japan, Russia, Saudi Arabia, the United Kingdom and the United States have 46 per cent of the voting rights in the World Bank and 48 per cent of the voting rights in the International Monetary Fund (IMF).

Source: UNDP, 2002

Women are less likely than men to be in paid employment. When employed, they are likely to earn less than men. They are more likely than men to work in the informal economy or in agriculture. But they have less access to finance, land and other resources to ensure decent earnings.

households, girls and women bore the brunt of the impact in terms of food. For example, the levels of malnutrition among pre-school and school-aged girls were higher than for boys. The birth weights of babies born to low-income mothers also declined.

There is no easy formula that a government can use to determine which budget allocation will have the maximum impact on poverty. However, it is relatively easy to see that some aspects of a budget – such as defence-related programmes

GRBs are a good way of supporting gender mainstreaming [which is] ... currently the main international approach to promoting equality between women and men.

Box 8: The Feminisation of Poverty

It is often said that 70 per cent of poor people are women, and the term 'feminisation of poverty' is widely used. This term can mean several different things, but it is not always clear which meaning is intended. To make good policy, it is important to be clear what is being talked about.

BRIDGE (2001) suggests that the term has at least three different meanings:

- Women have a higher incidence of poverty than men (i.e. a higher percentage of women than men are poor);

- Women's poverty is more severe than that of men (i.e. poor women are even poorer, on average, than poor men); and

- The rates or levels of poverty among women are increasing. This may be because of an increase in the number of female-headed households.

The first two meanings describe a 'state' in which women suffer more in some way from poverty than men. The last meaning describes a process through which women are becoming poorer over time, and doing so faster than men. The first two points are probably true in most countries. The third point may be, but is not always, true.

– will not assist with poverty reduction. For example, the US Women's Budget Project initiated by the Women's International League for Peace and Freedom (WILPF) in 1996 estimated that the money spent on funding the 'Sea wolf' attack submarine for one year ($1.7 billion) could have provided energy assistance for 5.6 million low-income households.

Supporting gender mainstreaming

GRBs are a good way of supporting gender mainstreaming. Gender mainstreaming is currently the main international approach to promoting equality between women and men. It aims to make all government policy-making and implementation gender-sensitive, rather than having separate programmes – in a separate 'stream' – that focus on women or gender (see box 9). This approach will, however, only succeed if sufficient human, financial and material resources are allocated to implement it. If these resources are not made available, gender-sensitive aspects of policies may be present on paper but will not happen in practice. GRBs focus on ensuring that the financial resources, in particular, are made available.

> *Box 9:* **Mainstreaming Gender in Ethiopia**
>
> In Ethiopia, a National Women's Affairs Policy was adopted in 1993. The policy proposed the establishment of Women Focal Points in each ministry both at federal and state levels. The main purpose of these focal points is to mainstream gender into the activities of each sector and authority, which includes engendering the budget. There is also a Women's Affairs Committee in parliament that is one of nine standing committees. The role of this committee is to see to it that every piece of legislation that is passed by parliament has incorporated the proper gender balance. In addition, the committee tries to monitor how effective the activities of various ministries and agencies are in gradually ensuring real gender equality.

The Commonwealth has promoted both GRBs and gender mainstreaming and was quick to see the synergies between them:

- Gender-sensitive budgets serve as a tool to monitor expenditure for the Commonwealth's gender management system (GMS), a system-wide approach to gender mainstreaming.

- Since budgets cover all government ministries and departments, GRBs provide a practical opportunity for officials across sectors to use gender analysis in their work.

- Since finance ministries play a key role in budget management and general government decision-making, GRBs help to introduce gender issues at the centre of government operations and financial management.

The inclusion of women's voices and a gender perspective in decision-making enhances the legitimacy of governance. It enriches political processes by contributing new skills, styles and visions.

Strengthening governance

The last decade has seen greater interest in improving governance through increased accountability, participation and transparency within government decision-making processes.

- Accountability refers to the way in which government accounts for itself to citizens – how it lets citizens know its decisions and how these decisions were made, as well as the actions that it takes as a result of the decisions.

- Participation refers to the extent to which citizens, particularly the poor and other vulnerable and excluded groups such as women, are involved in the government's decisions and actions.

- Transparency refers to the availability of information to citizens on all decisions and actions that are made by the government. It also refers to the government's efforts to make the information easily understood by all citizens.

Budgets are an ideal area in which to focus on governance. Local and national governments and civil society groups – as well as multilateral and bilateral agencies – have looked for ways to improve the governance of government budgets. This has happened, in particular, in countries undergoing decentralisation of government. Decentralisation is seen by many as having the possibility of increasing participation by the local community and local legislators in budget decision-making and promoting greater responsiveness to their needs. The inclusion of women's voices and a gender perspective in decision-making enhances the legitimacy of governance. It enriches political processes by contributing new skills, styles and visions (see box 10).

In reality, in most countries there have been few improvements in budget-related governance. Most governments work on the premise that budgets must be formulated in secret, away from the markets, consumers and opposition. They therefore continue to operate a closed-door policy throughout the budget process until the time it is tabled in parliament. There are, however, some exceptions. For example, the Ugandan government has established sector working groups that come together early in the budget process to discuss and plan policies

FOWODE's report, The Gender Budget 1998/99, *makes a gender analysis of sectoral budgets in Uganda.*

Box 10: Including Women in Decision-making Processes

In Uganda, the Forum for Women in Democracy (FOWODE) and its allies first focused its attention on getting a quota clause in the constitution. The clause ensured that at least 30 per cent of local government representatives were women. Winning this victory, however, was only the first step. FOWODE and its allies then worked to increase the capacity of the local women representatives to understand and promote gender equality. They developed a gender budget initiative that brought together local government officials, local women representatives, national members of parliament for the area, CSOs and academics to analyse the local government budgets.

In Bacolod City in the Philippines, the NGO Development through Active Women Networking (DAWN) Foundation first helped women stand for and fight local elections. As a result of DAWN's activities, the number of women councillors increased. The executive director of DAWN was one of the new councillors. She and her colleagues recognised the importance of budgets, and worked together with gender activists from two other cities in a GRB initiative. Soon after the research was finished, a leading member of DAWN who was one of the budget researchers became the city administrator – the top official in local government. She and her colleagues in DAWN and the administration are now working to implement the gender-sensitive policies and budgets that they advocated in their research.

Gender Budget Trail *tells the story of how women are working to implement a gender-sensitive budget in Bacolod City in the Philippines.*

and budgets. These groups include representatives of civil society groups that have knowledge of the particular sectors. FOWODE is one such group.

Even after budgets are tabled in parliament, there is often little opportunity for participation. In many countries legislators have very limited powers to change the budget numbers. Even where they have such powers, they sometimes do not have the will to use them because of their political allegiances.

Civil society [is] ... hampered by limited access to and the density of the available information. However, [it] is often the spark that gets government moving on GRB work and keeps initiatives going.

The Tanzania Gender Networking Programme's publication Budgeting with a Gender Focus *suggests that some of the money currently spent on perks for top officials should go to a girls' scholarship fund.*

Civil society has even fewer powers than parliament. It is also hampered by limited access to and the density of the available information. However, civil society is often the spark that gets government moving on GRB work and keeps initiatives going. For example:

- In Mexico, the policy research NGO Fundar has worked closely with the Department of Health to review its budgets and introduce gender criteria into its main framework. Fundar and its allies in the Mexican gender budget initiative have also reached out to other government departments, committees in Congress, the national women's machinery (NWM), and the media and other parts of civil society.

- In the United Kingdom, the Women's Budget Group maintains strong links with parliamentarians, the women's unit in government and the media as part of its continued strategy to influence the national budget.

- In Tanzania, the NGO Tanzanian Gender Networking Programme (TGNP) spearheaded work on GRBs. TGNP's research and advocacy inspired government, with donor support, to initiate its own gender budget work within the Ministry of Finance. Today, TGNP acts as a consultant to government on GRBs and is also a participant in budget-related processes such as the poverty reduction strategy paper (PRSP) and annual public expenditure reviews (PERs).

Monitoring and evaluating government spending

A series of UN conferences in the 1990s discussed the relationship between gender, political commitment, resource allocation and development. In 2000, governments agreed on the Millennium Development Goals (MDGs) to be reached by 2015. The MDGs include a number of goals relevant to gender, but these are not the only international and national commitments in terms of gender and development. As noted earlier, the Beijing Platform for Action (PFA) and Beijing + 5 Document, the Commonwealth Plan of Action on Gender and Development and regional action plans, among others, also include goals related to gender equality. Many countries have also drawn up their own gender policies and action plans.

Policy statements, plans and international agreements do not necessarily result in tangible outcomes, however. Some countries have made progress with their commitments, but progress has been slow in others, while in some countries there have been significant setbacks. One major cause of the limited progress is the recent economic crises in most parts of the world. Another common cause is insufficient allocation or ineffective use of public resources. GRBs provide a way of tracking government expenditures against the commitments made nationally, regionally and internationally to gender and development.

GRBs provide a way of tracking government expenditures against the commitments made nationally, regionally and internationally to gender and development.

2. Understanding the Context

What is a Government Budget?

One of the first challenges in getting involved in gender-responsive budgets is the need to understand what the government budget is and how, when and by whom it is drawn up and implemented. This is particularly important for people outside government who want to do research or advocacy, as people in civil society usually have little knowledge of the budget and budget process. But it is also important for people inside government to understand the wider context of budgeting. Understanding how government budgets work makes it possible to identify the strategic entry points that are most likely to lead to gender-sensitive changes to the budget. Understanding the process gives pointers as to how and where to begin and what particular groups of stakeholders need to be engaged at each point.

A government budget is a financial statement of the expected revenue and intended expenditure of the government over a given period, usually a year.

- *Revenue* is the money that government thinks it will receive during the budget period. It includes taxes, social security contributions, fees or charges for services and money from miscellaneous sources such as interest on government loans.

- *Expenditure* is the money that government intends to spend. It is made up of two parts:
  - *Current expenditure* includes spending on salaries for public servants, the provision of goods and services, social security (e.g. in the form of grants), subsidies and interest on the national debt. This is money that is usually allocated and spent within a given budget year.
  - *Capital expenditure* involves spending on infrastructure. These allocations can be spread over several budget years, as an infrastructure project may take more than a year to complete.

One of the first challenges in getting involved in gender-responsive budgets is the need to understand what the government budget is and how, when and by whom it is drawn up and implemented.

The government budget is not ... simply a technical instrument for compiling and reporting on government revenue and expenditure plans. It is the primary policy statement made by the government.

In some developing countries, the budget is divided in other ways. For example, many developing countries distinguish between: (a) the recurrent budget, which is mainly funded by money raised within the country; and (b) the development budget or public investment programme, which is mainly funded by loans and grants from donors. The recurrent budget often more or less matches non-project current expenditure, while the development budget covers capital and current expenditure related to donor projects. However, the exact division, and the names given to different divisions, differ from country to country. In addition, significant amounts of donor funding are often not fully and accurately reported in government budgets.

The government budget is not, however, simply a technical instrument for compiling and reporting on government revenue and expenditure plans. It is the primary policy statement made by the government. Budgets are necessary because meeting people's needs always requires more resources than are available. Budgets indicate which needs will be prioritised and – implicitly – which needs will not be met by government.

The budget is usually tabled in parliament by the Minister of Finance on budget day, along with a review of the country's macroeconomic situation. In many countries, the Minister also tables other documents that report on government's achievements over the past budget year and its plans for the coming year. The Minister's budget speech and the tabled documents together reflect the fundamental values underlying government policy. The budget outlines the government's view of the socio-economic state of the nation. It declares the government's fiscal, financial and economic objectives and its social and economic priorities.

The budget thus provides an excellent opportunity for judging the level of gender-responsiveness of government policy. However, most governments compile their budgets and the related reports with very few explicit mentions of gender. Judging gender-responsiveness then requires analysis to reveal the implicit gender implications. One of the objectives of GRB work is that governments begin compiling budget reports that are explicit about gender so that both government and other players can see clearly what is happening.

This relates back to the earlier point about good governance, namely that a government's budget is an important means of promoting transparency and accountability. Usually the government budget must be approved by the legislature before the money can be spent or the income raised. In this way, the government is accountable to the legislature and its committees. By providing a detailed account of planned expenditure, the government budget also notifies the general public of 'where the money goes', thereby increasing transparency. Finally, if budgets include information on past activities, expenditure and revenue, the information can be compared with the previous year's budget and so provide a regulating and disciplining framework within which government agencies must carry out their functions.

Crucial economic functions of the budget[2]

Beyond ensuring accountability of the government to the legislature for revenue and expenditure and serving as a mechanism for controlling spending, the budget has three crucial economic functions:

- allocation of resources;
- distribution of income and wealth;
- stabilisation of the economy.

These functions can be shared between different levels of government: national, sub-national and municipal. The budgets at all these levels need to be examined to provide a complete picture of what government is or is not doing.

Allocation of resources

This function relates to the provision of public goods and services by the government. All the goods and services in a country are produced by either the public sector, the formal and informal economic sectors, or the not-for-profit community and unpaid household care sectors. In allocating resources, the government must decide both the relative size of the public sector provision, as well as how available resources are to be divided among the various government policies, programmes

2 This section is adapted from Budlender and Sharp, 1998.

GRBs seek to uncover the impacts of resource allocations on women, men, girls and boys. It is important to have gender-disaggregated data in order to determine how different groups are affected.

and functions (e.g. administration, health, education and defence).

Allocations to some of these will benefit women and girls more than men and boys, and vice-versa. GRBs seek to uncover the impacts of resource allocations on women, men, girls and boys. It is important to have gender-disaggregated data in order to determine how different groups are affected.

Distribution of income and wealth

This function refers to the use of fiscal policy and the budget to try to redress inequalities in income and wealth distribution within the society. Governments have to make decisions as to what constitutes a 'fair' distribution between different groups.

While governments have sometimes shown concern over the inequalities between rich and poor households, they also need to pay attention to inequalities between women and men, and between different members of each household, as the more vulnerable members of households have less access to available resources. GRBs are premised on the assumption that there should be a 'fair' distribution of income and wealth.

Stabilisation of the economy

This function responds to the need for government budgets to promote a certain level of employment, public spending, economic growth, environmental sustainability and external balance. Stabilisation policy requires the use of economic, political and social judgements to determine which objectives are to be given priority and what are the acceptable rates of unemployment, interest, levels of debt and so on.

A GRB analysis requires an understanding of the ways in which macroeconomic policy, its theoretical framework and the assumptions that underpin the budget overlook gender issues, especially women's role in the household and community care economy.

Economic growth is not an end in itself but a means of increasing available resources to enhance household well-being and human development objectives. However, dominant economic models presume that these concerns need not be addressed directly. Instead they assume that problems of inequality and poverty will be resolved by the 'trickle down' benefits of growth. This has not been the case.

Budgets are not an 'end' in themselves either. Therefore, the first task in preparing a budget should be to determine the policies and objectives that the budget is aiming to achieve. Budgets should follow policy rather than vice versa. If the policy is flawed, then the budget cannot be effective.

Medium-term expenditure frameworks

Over recent years, many governments have started drawing up medium-term expenditure frameworks (MTEFs). While the government budget usually covers a single year, the MTEF provides for plans and budgets over a longer period, usually three to five years. An MTEF encourages government to think ahead and make longer-term plans. It is useful for legislators and civil society actors who want to monitor government and engage in advocacy as it gives early information about government's future plans.

MTEFs are often introduced together with some form of programme or performance budgeting. The aim of programme budgeting it to make a stronger link between policy, planning and budgeting. The goal is for budgets to follow policy, rather than policies following budgets.

MTEFs are designed to correct the current situation in many countries where planning and budgeting take place independently of each other. Planning is often confined to investment or capital expenditures. Recurrent expenditures meanwhile change very little from year to year, except for adjustments for inflation. The separate treatment of recurrent and capital expenditures is exacerbated by the fact that the capital, development or public investment programme (PIP) budget is often funded by donors and has different accounting and utilisation guidelines from the recurrent budget.

In a typical MTEF process, government line agencies (ministries, departments and other institutions that deliver services) identify their specific objectives for the given period. Then they plan the activities needed to achieve the objectives, identify the inputs required, cost the activities and devise targets and indicators of output (delivery). Each agency is required to prioritise its objectives and activities on the basis of the government's overall social and economic objectives. The Finance Ministry or planning agency is then usually responsible for

Economic growth is not an end in itself but a means of increasing available resources to enhance household well-being and human development objectives.

In countries that take participation seriously, governments provide opportunities for citizens to have an input at different stages of the [budget] cycle.

overall prioritisation and ensuring that total spending is within the available 'envelope' of resources.

The linking of objectives, activities, targets and indicators is part of the 'performance' aspect of MTEFs. It is useful for advocates as these state explicitly what the government hopes to do, and provide explicit measures of what has been delivered.

Understanding the Budget Process

The budget process consists of a cycle. The details differ from country to country, but in most countries the cycle includes the steps shown in Figure 3. The figure focuses on activities by government. In countries that take participation seriously, governments provide opportunities for citizens to have an input at different stages of the cycle.

The actors shown in Figure 3 should ideally all be part of a single team working towards a common national interest. In reality, however, they often have different interests and can sometimes be in conflict. These differences need to be recog-

Figure 3: The Budget Cycle

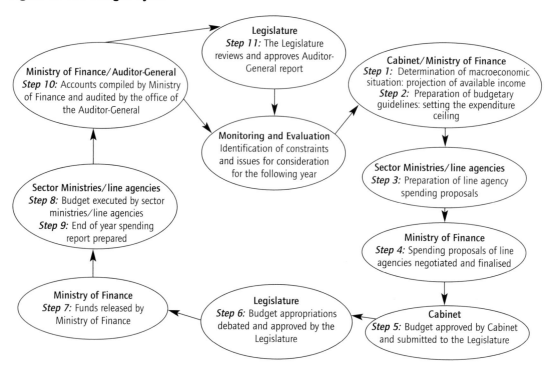

nised when trying to bring together the various stakeholders to collaborate on GRB initiatives.

The key steps of the budget process in most countries are:

- Determining the macroeconomic situation;
- Preparing budget guidelines and setting expenditure ceilings;
- Preparing sector ministry spending proposals;
- Securing legislative approval;
- Monitoring, evaluation and accountability.

Determining the macroeconomic situation

Before a government can draw up a budget, it must know what resources are available to it. Government projects (estimates) its available resources by looking at the macroeconomic situation, usually with the help of a model. This macroeconomic model looks at elements such as:

- The expected output (production) of the economy;
- The budget deficit (the difference between expenditure and revenue);
- The balance of payments (which measures foreign currency);
- The exchange rate (the value of the local currency in relation to foreign currencies);
- The availability of credit for loans.

How much money a government has available depends on economic and political choices. Government can, for example, increase revenue by increasing taxation. It can also choose by how much expenditure will exceed revenue in the year ahead, i.e. how big the deficit will be.

There are, however, constraints on the choices. This is particularly the case for governments in developing countries that are dependent on foreign aid and loans. In terms of revenue, governments have some control over the level of taxation. However, even here they worry that high corporate taxes will discourage investment, and that high levels of personal tax will alienate middle class voters. In terms of deficit, the structural

Planting rice.

INTERNATIONAL LABOUR ORGANIZATION/
J. MAILLARD

adjustment and stabilisation programmes of the 1980s and 1990s required that governments cut their budget deficits through reducing expenditure. More recently, multilateral agencies such as the IMF and World Bank, as well as bilateral donors, have set limits on the deficit and other macroeconomic indicators as a precondition for receiving loans, debt reduction and other forms of assistance.

Cabinet has the overall responsibility for ensuring that the budget meets the economic and social objectives of the country. In meeting this responsibility, it determines the priorities, sets the spending levels and proposes the allocations to sectors. Cabinet usually makes these decisions based on advice from the Finance Ministry, Central Bank and planning agency. It usually focuses on approving major changes in resource allocation, particularly new or expanding programmes or those that must be reduced. The Finance Ministry usually makes the decisions about other, smaller changes.

Preparing budget guidelines and setting expenditure ceilings

The Finance Ministry plays a central role in the budget process of most countries. It has the main responsibility for financial management and economic affairs, and has a lot of influence on Cabinet decision-making. The relationship between the Finance Ministry and sector ministries can be one of conflict. While the sector ministries want as much money for themselves as possible, the Finance Ministry must balance the demands of all the ministries at the same time as it controls total spending.

The first step in the budget process is to provide a realistic estimate of available revenue. On the basis of this estimate, the Finance Ministry or planning agency decides on an overall 'ceiling' (maximum) for total expenditure, as well as a ceiling for each sector ministry or spending agency. The Finance Ministry then distributes budget guidelines to each ministry, specifying its expenditure ceiling and how the budget should be prepared. Sector ministries then prepare budget proposals on the basis of these guidelines.

The expenditure ceilings should be based on the government's overall social and economic objectives. For example, if the country has a poverty reduction strategy paper, the ceilings should follow its priorities. However, the Finance Ministry must also take into consideration a number of budgetary commitments (Foster and Fozzard, 2000). These include:

- Statutory commitments such as transfers to sub-national government, welfare and pension entitlements, and revenue-expenditure for other special funds;

- Contractual commitments to pay public servants;

- Debt servicing;

- Contracts for the delivery of goods and services ordered in previous budget periods;

- Agreements with multilateral and bilateral agencies to pay a certain share of externally-funded projects and programmes.

The expenditure ceilings should be based on the government's overall social and economic objectives. For example, if the country has a poverty reduction strategy paper, the ceilings should follow its priorities.

> ### *Box 11:* The Changing Role of Finance Ministries
>
> In the past, planning ministries played the lead role in many countries in determining overall policy direction, while finance ministries played a supportive role. At that time, it was the task of the Planning Ministry to set the strategic direction, structure and pattern of economic growth, distribution of income and employment, creation of physical infrastructure, human development and poverty alleviation. In doing so, the Planning Ministry coordinated and balanced the strategic plans of the sector ministries and worked with the Finance Ministry to ensure the financial viability of these plans.
>
> The roles and the division of labour between finance and planning ministries began to change with the introduction of structural adjustment-oriented economic reforms. Because these reforms placed great emphasis on 'fiscal discipline' and on controlling the level of expenditure, the role of finance ministries changed from a supportive one to a disciplining one. In the words of Gita Sen: "Ministries are now required to cut their coats according to their financial cloth, and it is the Finance Ministry that determines how much cloth there is".
>
> Adapted from Sen, 1999

Preparing sector ministry spending proposals

The next step is for the sector ministries to draw up detailed proposals as to how they will spend the money allocated in their 'ceiling'. In most countries, ministries do this as an internal process. However, in a few countries governments have opened up the process to get input from others – for example, the sector working groups in Uganda mentioned earlier.

After the ministries have submitted their proposals, the Finance Ministry has separate meetings with each to negotiate. As with the overall ceiling, sector ministry proposals should match the country's overall objectives, as well as sector-specific plans. However, very often the ministries submit spending proposals that are simply based on the previous year's budget, perhaps with adjustments for inflation. In other cases, they submit proposals that are way above the ceilings, in the hope that the large bids will convince the Finance Ministry of the extent of the demand.

Where the proposals are over the ceiling, the discussions focus on where they can be cut. The pitfall with overly large estimates is that they are likely to be interpreted as a sign that the sector ministry is not serious, or has not got the capacity to do its own planning. Since the Finance Ministry usually does not understand the sector as well as the Ministry concerned, it may cut programmes that the Ministry considers important. Sector officials can then become despondent and lose commitment.

Cuts can also happen at this stage even where proposals are within the ceilings. This happens, for example, when multilateral institutions have convinced the Finance Ministry that its original estimates of revenue were too high, or its planned deficit too large.

Securing legislative approval

In most countries, government expenditure and revenue raising require some legal authorisation. The Cabinet and Ministry of Finance draw up budget proposals, but the legislature – as the representatives of the people – must usually approve these proposals before they become legally enforceable (see box 12).

The primary function of the legislature in the budget process is to pass the Budget Act. This provides the opportunity for legislators to scrutinise, discuss and decide on the acceptability of the government's proposals. However, legislative scrutiny may be inadequate for a number of reasons:

- There is insufficient time for scrutiny and debate of the budget;

- The required information for analysis of the budget may be absent;

- Legislators may lack the capacity, resources or will to analyse the budget;

- Legislative powers regarding the budget may be limited;

- The government may have too much influence over legislative decision-making;
- A limited number of special interest groups may have too much power, and reduce the ability of legislators to focus the budget on achieving the nation's priority goals.

> ### Box 12: Legislative Powers to Amend Budgets
>
> The legal powers of the legislature to amend the budget vary from one country to another. Three situations are common:
>
> 1. *Unrestricted power.* In these countries, the legislature can vary both expenditure and revenue either up or down without the consent of the government. Presidential systems fit this model, although the president usually has the final veto.
>
> 2. *Restricted power.* In these countries, the legislature can amend the budget, but only within set limits (e.g. it may only be able to decrease or increase expenditure or revenue by a certain percentage). The extent of the restrictions varies from country to country. In the United Kingdom, France and many Commonwealth countries, legislatures cannot propose amendments that increase expenditures. In Germany, the legislature can propose increases, but these must be approved by the government.
>
> 3. *Balanced budget power.* In these countries, the legislature can raise or lower expenditure or revenue, but must always propose other increases or decreases that keep the total revenue and expenditure the same. In this system, the legislature has the power to change priorities but cannot change totals.
>
> In some countries, the legislature has virtually no powers at all over budgets. The legislature must accept the budget as is or reject it completely. Legislatures are usually very reluctant to totally reject a budget as this would cause the government to fall and require a new election.
>
> Adapted from Shiavo-Campo *et al.*, 1999

After passing the Budget Act, legislators are also responsible for overseeing the execution of the budget. They do this with the assistance of bodies such as the Office of the Auditor-General (OAG). However, as noted above, oversight and monitoring is often limited by the availability and quality of information provided.

Monitoring, evaluation and accountability

Ideally, the budget cycle should contain a feedback loop that allows for lessons learned from current budgets to inform future budget preparation and execution. In terms of monitoring and evaluation, there need to be checks on whether the money was spent as planned. Cases of over-expenditure raise questions about where the money came from – which programmes lost out so that this programme could spend more. Cases of under-expenditure raise questions about delivery – which potential beneficiaries did not receive services because government did not spend the money as allocated, and what were the reasons for under-expenditure.

In addition to comparing the monetary amount of actual expenditure vs. planned expenditure, performance budgeting allows for a comparison of actual delivery output vs. planned targets – for example, how many pupils were taught, how many patients were treated in hospitals and clinics, or how many houses were provided with electricity and water. This type of monitoring is intended to measure efficiency and effectiveness. If outputs and targets are disaggregated, for example by gender or region, it can also measure equity.

The Office of the Auditor-General is government's auditor and plays a critical role in the chain of public accountability between the government and the public. The OAG should be independent of other government agencies. It assists the legislature in overseeing the management of public funds by providing independent assessments of, and advice about, how sector ministries have used the resources allocated to them. The role of the Auditor-General is often described as ensuring that government provides 'value for money' by using the available resources efficiently and economically. The OAG should also, however, be reporting on whether the money is spent equitably.

Ideally, the budget cycle should contain a feedback loop that allows for lessons learned from current budgets to inform future budget preparation and execution. In terms of monitoring and evaluation, there need to be checks on whether the money was spent as planned.

In reality, monitoring and evaluation by the OAG is often not as thorough as one would wish. In many countries, the Auditor-General's reports are only released more than a year after the budget year has ended. At that stage, they are of little use for informing future budgets. In addition, monitoring and evaluation of the previous year's results can be inhibited by lack of data at different points in the budget cycle. In particular, when governments introduce programme or performance budgeting, they are usually quite good at specifying targets for the year ahead, but very poor at reporting on what was delivered in previous years. The OAG is sometimes denied information because sector ministries or individuals within them want to hide their actions. In some cases, they are hiding inefficiencies and inequities. In other cases, they are hiding outright corruption.

Box 13: Citizen Participation in the Budget Process in Porto Alegre, Brazil

As seen in Figure 3, the key players in the budget process are the legislature, the Cabinet, the Finance Ministry and sector ministries. Ideally, civil society should also be a key player. This is not currently the case in most parts of the world, but there are a few exceptions.

Porto Alegre, a large industrial city in Brazil with 1.3 million inhabitants, is the most well known of a number of experiments by the country's Workers' Party to involve ordinary citizens in formulating city budgets. Here, the mayor's office acts as the local government and the Chamber of Deputies as the legislature. The mayor's office prepares the budget, which then has to be approved by the Chamber.

To facilitate citizen participation, the city is divided into sixteen regions, and topics for discussion are divided into five themes: (i) transport; (ii) education, leisure and culture; (iii) health and social welfare; (iv) economic development and taxation; and (v) city organisation and urban development. Two rounds of plenary meetings in each region and on each theme are held every year.

Box 13(*continued*)

The first step in the annual process occurs around March. Citizens' meetings are held, without any participation by the mayor's office, to gather the demands of citizens and select regional delegates. The next step is a round of meetings in April between the citizens and the mayor's office, including the mayor. Participants in these meetings review the investment plans of the previous year, discuss proposals for the next year and elect people to the Forum of Delegates, which takes discussions further. Between March and June, the mayor's office also holds informal preparatory meetings with community associations to discuss demands for investment in different sectors. These demands are ranked on a scale of 1 to 5 by the participants. The rankings are then aggregated by the mayor's office together with points allocated according to: (a) need; and (b) population size.

A second round of meetings takes place in July when two councillors are elected from each of the 16 regions and from each of the five themes. Together with a member each from the civil servants' trade union and an umbrella organisation of neighbourhood communities, these representatives make up a 44-member Council of Participatory Budgeting (COP). These councillors study and debate criteria for resource allocation and citizen demands and on this basis revise the budget proposal prepared by the mayor's planning office and the mayor's cabinet. At the end of September, they submit a final budget proposal to the legislature.

Between September and December, the COP follows the budget debates in the Chamber and lobbies intensely for its proposals. It also draws up a detailed investment plan that specifies the public works to be undertaken and corresponding allocations for each region.

Adapted from World Bank Participation and Civic Engagement website:
http://www.worldbank.org/participation/

3. Implementing a Gender-responsive Budget

Learning about the Situation in a Particular Country

The previous section provided a general overview of the institutional arrangements of budget formulation, execution and accounting. Anyone beginning gender budget work needs to learn about the particular institutional arrangements and process in their own country. This involves asking the following key questions:

- What are the formal procedures for budget formulation, execution and accounting?

- Have there been recent attempts to change the budget process, format or institutional arrangements?

- Which macroeconomic models does the government use in the first steps of the budget process?

- Which policy papers and processes determine the national priorities that should determine budget allocations?

- What constraints – such as legal requirements to have a balanced budget, donor conditionalities, expenditure reduction or deficit reduction – does the government consider in formulating the budget?

- In what format is the budget presented? Are allocations arranged according to programmes or according to accounting categories such as salaries, materials or travel? Does the budget contain information about objectives, activities, targets and indicators? Does the budget contain information about the previous year's performance in terms of money and delivery? Does government produce a medium-term expenditure framework that shows planned expenditure for longer than one year?

- What is the role of central agencies such as the Finance Ministry and planning agency in budget preparation and execution?

Groups working on GRBs need to have the technical skills both to understand government budgets and to apply a gender perspective to them. Advocacy and negotiation skills are also important in any attempt to influence budgets.

- How much of government expenditure is allocated for servicing debt?

- What are the role and powers of the legislature in budget formulation and oversight? How effective is the legislature in these roles?

- What are the role and powers of the Auditor-General? How effective is the Auditor-General?

- Where there are sub-national governments, what powers do they possess with regard to revenue raising or expenditure allocation? For what functions/sectors of government are they responsible?

- Are there any civil society groups involved in budget work?

In asking these questions, it is useful to ask about both the theory (what is meant to happen) and the practice (what actually happens). In some countries there are good policies and procedures on paper, but they are not always followed.

Issues Affecting the Sustainability of Gender Budget Work

The following are some of the important considerations in undertaking gender budget work. They are adapted from a list developed by the Swedish International Development Cooperation Agency (Sida) (Stark and de Vylder, 1998).

Skills

Groups working on GRBs need to have the technical skills both to understand government budgets and to apply a gender perspective to them. Advocacy and negotiation skills are also important in any attempt to influence budgets. Groups can increase their skills through consulting resource materials, collaborating with organisations with experience in the budget and gender fields, and contact with gender budget groups in other countries. Groups can also increase their skills by jumping in at the deep end and experimenting themselves.

Time

One-off initiatives are unlikely to have a significant impact on the budget, unless conditions are very favourable for a particular budget change. Workshops, in particular, will not usually achieve sustainable impact unless they are followed up by further action. Groups that engage in gender budget work should be prepared to commit time, energy and other resources for at least three years.

Flexibility and adaptability

Gender budget work is a relatively new area of work and there is no single blueprint or model for implementation. Also, because the structure and priorities of budgets differ from country to country, each initiative needs to be shaped to the country in which it occurs. Where groups borrow tools and methods from others, they will need to modify them to fit their own circumstances.

Support

Groups involved in gender budget work may require support to implement or develop their programme. There are a number of agencies that have provided financial and other support to these initiatives in the past (see box 20).

Follow-up

GRB analysis is not an end in itself. The analysis provides information on how budgets affect women and men, girls and boys, and other groups. In order for gender budget work to be meaningful to ordinary people, groups need to have a strategy to take forward the issues that emerge from their analysis.

Who Could be Involved in a GRB Initiative?

In different countries, different players have been involved in GRB initiatives. Who is involved depends, in part, on who starts the initiative, what their objectives are and who they target as allies and key stakeholders. Who is involved also shapes the nature of the initiative and the activities undertaken.

Civil society

Beginning in the 1990s, there has been a significant growth in interest among civil society groups around government budgets. The term 'civil society' refers to a range of groupings in society that participate in some way in public life. It thus

Beginning in the 1990s, there has been a significant growth in interest among civil society groups around government budgets.

includes not only NGOs but also other civil society organisations such as professional associations, research and policy centres, philanthropic foundations and community-based groups. The media, business organisations and trade unions also make up part of civil society.

A number of these different agencies have been involved in outside-government GRB initiatives. In fact, there are now civil society GRB initiatives in over two dozen countries. This growth has been matched by a rapid expansion in other types of independent budget groups (see box 14). Some of them work mainly as think tanks, and may even act as advisors to government. Some aim to make budget information more widely accessible and understandable, while others have advocacy as their main objective. In general, however, these groups have ignored gender issues.

In a few cases groups have tried to formulate comprehensive budgets as an alternative to those offered by the government. For example, in 1995, the Canadian Centre on Policy Alternatives started an Alternative Federal Budget exercise. The more common approach is for civil society groups to analyse government budgets without proposing a comprehensive alternative. The critiques are then presented to government, the legislature and the public with the hope of bringing about specific changes. While some groups focus broadly on the poor, others have looked at specific vulnerable groups such as people with disabilities, the environment, youth or children (see box 15).

Australian GRB is often cited to illustrate the limitations of such initiatives if civil society is not involved. The Australian experience provides support for the argument that one reason for the limited action by government in the area of gender and development is the weakness of public pressure.

Civil society and governments work most easily together on GRB initiatives when there is broad agreement between them on the need for gender equality. In such cases, the gender advocates in government usually welcome the pressure from outside groups, while the civil society groups rely on their allies in government for access to information and influence. Joint work is also facilitated if there is broad political agreement between the different players and an acceptance of their different roles and rights.

Box 14: Some Reasons for the Growth in Budget Work

The growth in independent budget groups reflects several international developments. These include:

Democratisation: Budget work frequently flourishes in countries undergoing a democratic transition such as Indonesia, Russia, South Africa and Uganda. Greater democracy allows civil society and legislatures to play a bigger role in public policy, which stimulates a demand for greater transparency. A virtuous cycle is created, deepening democracy.

Decentralisation: Recent years have also seen increasing decentralisation in many countries. This may happen together with democratisation or for other reasons. Decentralisation has the potential of opening opportunities for greater participation in budget-making by members of local communities. On the other hand, it makes monitoring what is happening to budgets and public money at a national level more complicated. This is because there are more budgets to monitor, and because different local governments may use different formats and methods of budgeting. Decentralisation can also increase inequalities between regions if the national government does not provide sufficient transfers and assistance to compensate for differences in their wealth.

Public expenditure management: Independent budget institutions have emerged in a period when many countries are introducing significant changes in the way they budget. In particular, the new public expenditure management methods show more clearly how budgets are linked to policy, as well as what is to be delivered by different programmes. The new methods provide better information, which allows for better oversight and monitoring by civil society and legislatures. Medium-term expenditure frameworks provide information over a longer period, allowing greater time for lobbying.

Box 14 (continued)

International financial institutions and poverty alleviation: Independent budget work is also increasingly supported by international financial institutions (IFIs) such as the World Bank and IMF, as well as by other multilateral institutions and bilateral donors. These agencies acknowledge that there has been little progress in addressing poverty and inequality in the developing world in recent decades. They believe that there is a role for civil society actors, both private sector and others, in achieving development. Civil society budget work is seen as one way that this can happen.

Adapted from Krafchik, 2002

Non-governmental organisations

The term 'NGO' is broad and obscures important differences between the actors across and within countries. In Mexico, for example, the core NGOs in the GRB initiative are a policy research organisation and a women's organisation. In South Africa, the two core NGOs are both policy research organisations, but they have drawn on a wide range of other NGOs, including some gender advocacy organisations. In Tanzania and Uganda, it is women's or gender organisations that are leading the initiatives. In the Philippines, the civil society initiative involves two local women's organisations, one 'mixed' people's organisation and a national gender network. Each of the different types of organisations has strengths and weaknesses. Initiatives are probably most successful when the core organisations are able to link up with other 'types' of civil society organisations that complement them.

In many countries, unfortunately, there is an antagonistic relationship between NGOs and government. While governments are often suspicious of NGOs, NGOs similarly often have hesitations about engaging too closely with government. They are sometimes sceptical of government's real commitment to gender equality. They may also be concerned about co-option, loss of critical distance and being used by government

Box 15: Case Studies: Two Projects Examining Expenditure – on Children (South Africa) and on Tribal People (India)

1. The Children's Budget Project in South Africa

The Children's Budget Project (CBP) is housed in the NGO Institute for Democracy in South Africa (IDASA). The CBP does not argue for a separate budget for children. Rather, it examines the link between government policy commitments to children and government budget allocations. In particular, it examines whether government is fulfilling its constitutional commitment to 'put children first'. The CBP's intended audience includes CSOs, government departments and legislatures. Its research findings are disseminated as widely as possible through publications, radio, newspapers, the project's website, and training and workshops conducted by project staff.

In its first phase, the CBP teamed up with other stake-holders in the children's sector to produce the report *First Call: The South African Children's Budget*. The study tracks government expenditure on children in areas such as health, education, welfare, justice and policing. CBP's second study, *Where Poverty Hits Hardest*, examines the link between government spending on social services aimed at children and children's ability to access these services in all nine provinces from 1995 to 1998. The CBP's third study focuses on government's performance in addressing child poverty through allocations to its poverty alleviation strategy.

The CBP has established itself as an important source of information on children's policy in South Africa. The report *First Call* was attached to the government's first report on the Convention on the Rights of the Child. The Project has also assisted government departments and CSOs requiring budget information on children.

Adapted from International Budget Project, 2000

2. Monitoring the Budget in Gujarat, India

The state of Gujarat is home to almost a tenth of India's 80 million tribal people. In 1992, the NGO Development Initiatives for Social and Human Action (DISHA) began to investigate what was happening to funds allotted under the Tribal Area Sub-plan. After obtaining copies of the budget, DISHA rearranges the data under different headings and enters them into a computer. Three questions are asked: (i) Does the budget mention specific pro-poor policies?; (ii) Are these policies supported by adequate funding allocations?; and (iii) Do the allocations fit the socio-economic reality of the Gujarati poor – the tribals, dalits, women and agricultural labourers? The day after the budget speech, the DISHA team briefs the press on its answers to these questions.

When discussions start in the legislature, DISHA feeds members of the legislative assembly (MLAs) with information briefs on a daily basis. The 4–5 page briefs are designed to assist legislators in demanding explanations from the government. Typically they cover: (a) general information about the department and the amount it received for spending; (b) the percentage changes in budget allocations for items; (c) examples of fiscal indiscipline and mathematical errors; and (d) new items or expenditure proposals.

Information on the budgets is also disseminated in local languages through newspapers and one-page fact sheets to tribal villages and schools. As part of its on-the-ground monitoring of budget implementation, DISHA writes to village authorities in tribal areas to ask about progress on construction works included in previous budgets. By analysing public expenditures in terms of what was promised and what was delivered to disadvantaged groups, DISHA assists communities in articulating demands and creating pressure for accountability in the public expenditure system.

Adapted from World Bank Participation and Civic Engagement website:
http://www.worldbank.org/participation/

or donors. Often this antagonism centres on resources, as both government and NGOs are dependent on the same donors. Sometimes the NGO-government antagonism can be lessened through working together. However, this is easier when there is common ground on which to build (see box 16).

When government or the party in power is wary of criticism, GRB initiatives face particular difficulties. In some cases, opposition parties may attempt to co-opt the GRB work. This may be acceptable to the GRB group if they see themselves as part of the opposition. However, it can cause the government to ignore the findings and advocacy.

> ### Box 16: NGO/Government Collaboration in Tanzania
>
> In Tanzania, NGOs have worked particularly closely with government on the latter's gender budget work. The Tanzania Gender Networking Programme has, in fact, acted as government's primary consultant on gender-responsive budgeting. In this role it has trained budget officials on how to integrate gender into their MTEFs and budgets, and has conducted workshops for finance and planning officials on integrating gender into macroeconomic models. TGNP is also a regular participant in meetings around the annual public expenditure reviews and monitoring of the PRSP. This unusually close collaboration between NGOs and the government is a result of trust that has been built over time.

Some budget groups attempt to avoid choosing political sides by presenting their work as purely technical. The balance between 'technical' and 'political' depends on strategic choices that, in turn, depend on the particular situation in a country, the actors involved and the objectives of the GRB initiative. The balancing act is never easy, but is easier to manage if the group is clear about its strategy.

Gender and development organisations

Organisations that focus on women's and gender issues, whether at the sub-national, national or international levels, have been in the vanguard of gender budget work. This is not surprising as they have the experience, commitment and gender skills necessary to take the lead on these types of initiatives. However, the requirement in gender budget initiatives for skills in collaborating with governments or undertaking economic analysis has meant that many of the organisations that are normally at the forefront of work on gender and development (GAD) have been absent. While the lack of skills may have been an initial limitation, however, it has proved to be a strength to the programme as it has required many GAD organisations to build partnerships with groups that they have not traditionally worked with.

The grassroots

Few initiatives have succeeded in reaching the grassroots, although some claim to have done so. Often the term 'grassroots' is used in a loose way, for example, to refer to anyone who lives in a rural area. True grassroots and poor people are usually unorganised and marginalised, and may have little time or energy to spare for civic engagement. It is thus probably naïve to expect that they can easily be reached and motivated to participate in these initiatives. In general it is the local level initiatives that have gone 'deepest'. For example, the MKSS mobilised the poor in Rajasthan, India (see box 17) and the Tanzanian and Ugandan initiatives have obtained information from, and discussed issues with, ordinary people. The Karnataka initiative in India builds on past participatory work at the local level, but the direct participants are local women leaders rather than 'ordinary grassroots' citizens. Similarly, the Asia Foundation's initiatives in the Philippines and Indonesia work with locally organised women and leaders. The South African development of workshop materials is intended to assist community-based groups in using the techniques and learning of gender budget analysis and advocacy. The original materials have since been adapted, with appropriate examples, for use in Botswana and Zimbabwe.

Box 17: Case study: Grassroots Organising around Budgets (India)

In the early 1990s, a mass-based organisation called the Mazdoor (labour) Kisan (farmer) Shakti (strength) Sangathan (organisation) (MKSS) started working in one of the most neglected areas of Rajasthan, India. Members of the core group went from village to village asking a simple question: Did the people know how much money was coming to their village for development and where it was being spent? This was a simple question the poor could understand but had not dared to ask before.

The MKSS went to the government administration to request detailed information on development expenditure. They were told there was no government rule allowing villagers to have this information. To penetrate this 'Iron Curtain' between the community and the government, the MKSS launched a people's campaign – the biggest public campaign since the Freedom Movement in the 1940s. The campaign included public hearings where villagers shared stories of corruption with several thousand people. Other activities included sit-in protests and strikes.

In response to these protests, government established a Committee on Transparency to investigate whether it was feasible to supply photocopies of bills, vouchers and other documents to the public. When the Committee found it was possible, the state government declared the findings secret. However, after a 53-day strike the Deputy Chief Minister revealed that a Gazette (government order) had been published allowing access to public documents six months before the strike started.

The MKSS then decided to test the power of this Gazette. At first, the local officials said they did not know anything about it. When the MKSS showed them a copy of the Gazette, they refused to obey it until additional MKSS organising activities forced them to do so. To exert pressure, the MKSS held a series of public hearings at which it shared its experience with local people. The first

NGOs tend to commission academics to assist with the work because they feel that they do not have the necessary skills. One danger of this approach is that the NGO does not play a strong enough role in directing and overseeing the research.

Box 17 (*continued*)

meeting resulted in one official returning 100,000 rupees that she had embezzled. The second meeting resulted in 147,000 and 114,000 rupees being returned by two other officials. It was not fear of the law or official disciplinary action that made the officials return the money. It was fear of the people through the public hearings that finally forced them to do so.

Adapted from Bunker, 2000

Academics

Some initiatives draw on academics, particularly for research purposes. Some have academics at the forefront. NGOs tend to commission academics to assist with the work because they feel that they do not have the necessary skills. One danger of this approach is that the NGO does not play a strong enough role in directing and overseeing the research. Academic research usually allows for quite a lot of latitude in choosing the topic and shaping it to the readily available evidence and theory. Policy-advocated research, on the other hand, requires that the researcher stick to the topic no matter how difficult it is to find the necessary facts. A second danger is that the NGO members might not understand the research well enough to use it effectively in advocacy and argument if they have not done it themselves.

In Tanzania, TGNP attempted to address some of these issues in the first years by having project teams made up of academics, NGO representatives and government officials. More recently, it has decided to use its own staff and members as researchers. In the Philippines, DAWN at first planned to commission an academic to do the research for them. They subsequently reversed this decision and did it themselves, despite limited previous research experience. In retrospect, they were pleased with their strategy, as it placed them in an excellent position to use their findings in advocacy on the City Council and in training others.

In training, the use of academics can have both advantages

and disadvantages. In some cases, government officials respect academics more than NGO representatives. In others, the academics are seen as impractical, theoretical and difficult to understand.

Individuals

Most CSOs that take on GRB work are already engaged in a range of other activities. Unless one or two individuals in the organisation see the budget work as their special responsibility and passion, it can easily be neglected. Similarly, when the initiative is undertaken by a network of organisations, it is important that one of these organisations take responsibility for driving it forward.

Ideally, however, GRB initiatives should not be reliant on the presence of individuals. Where they are, there is a danger that the initiative will die when the key players move on.

Men

Gender is about the relations between male and female people. However, most gender budget initiatives tend to focus on women. This is understandable, given that it is predominantly women and girls who are disadvantaged in gender relationships.

Nevertheless, in several countries men have been key players in GRB initiatives. To some extent, this can be expected, given the dominance of men in the economic fields. In African and South Asian initiatives in particular, there have often been men among the researchers as there are relatively few female economists. Across countries men have also featured as the 'target group' for lobbying and training in inside-government initiatives because of the dominant role they play in budgetary decision-making.

The Ugandan example, however, raises the question of the extent to which men should be considered 'targets' in non-governmental initiatives. FOWODE argues that working with women separately is often better in order to build confidence and assertiveness.

The media

The media can be very influential in promoting demands for changes in government policy, programmes and budgets. Its potential depends on its level of independence from political

Ideally ... GRB initiatives should not be reliant on the presence of individuals. Where they are, there is a danger that the initiative will die when the key players move on.

The media can be very influential in promoting demands for changes in government policy, programmes and budgets. Its potential depends on its level of independence from political influence.

influence. In some countries the media can be a strong mechanism to ensure transparency and accountability on the part of government. Politicians and officials are usually sensitive to public criticism and media reporting on the ineffectiveness or misuse of public funds, which can increase the chances of changes being introduced. The potential is greatest where the media is free to be critical of government policy and can provide analytical coverage of economic and budgetary issues and debates. In these cases, groups involved in GRB work can use the media to disseminate their viewpoints to the wider public. However, in many countries the state has significant influence in the press and complete or near-complete control of radio and television. In these countries, the media might refuse to publish even mild criticism of government actions.

Government

The government executive

Budgets are inherently political. Because the available resources are always less than enough to meet all demands, politicians allocate the available money according to their understanding of the various needs and preferences within the society, as well as their understanding of the power of different groups.

Some GRB initiatives were clearly driven by strong political dynamics. The Australian Women's Budget was born after the mid-1980s Labour Party victory. The South African Women's Budget Initiative started after the first democratic elections of 1994 and the commitment of the African National Congress (ANC) to establish a non-racist and non-sexist society. In the UK, after its election victory in the late 1990s, New Labour provided the opportunity for the UK Women's Budget Group to meet with the Treasury to discuss gender issues related to budget policy. The key change that led to the formation of the Engender Women's Budget Group in Scotland was the establishment of the devolved Scottish Parliament in May 1999. The Rwandan initiative is occurring in the context of a new, post-genocide government attempting to reconstruct the country.

The success of a GRB initiative in effecting a change in

government budget policy or allocations will depend on the degree of political support that it can attract from the highest levels of government: from ministers of finance, from gender ministers and from their cabinet colleagues. Support from top officials is also important, as they provide technical and policy advice to the ministers.

The Rwandan gender budget initiative was officially launched by the Prime Minister at a ceremony attended by virtually all the ministers and secretary-generals of line ministries. This public show of support for the initiative encouraged the Finance Ministry and sector ministry officials who attended the subsequent training to take the exercise seriously. In the Gauteng Province of South Africa, the GRB initiative has been spearheaded by the Office of the Premier. The Premier is comparable to the Prime Minister of a country, and this office is thus the apex for policy-making in the province. Officials of the Premier's Office have worked closely with top finance officials in deciding on the shape and format of the gender budget statements to be produced (see also box 3).

The Finance Ministry

The discussion of the budget cycle above reveals the central role of the Finance Ministry. Most inside-government GRB initiatives have focused on the Finance Ministry because of the realisation that, to be effective, they need to be implemented in the context of the annual budget cycle. In addition to the necessary technical skill, the Finance Ministry has the political influence to mobilise support for GRBs if it so desires.

In Tanzania, the first phase of the inside-government gender budget initiative was driven by the Budget Office in the Ministry of Finance. This was a strategic location because this office establishes the systems for budgeting, and trains and supports officials in sector ministries in drawing up their budgets. The initiative had the strong support of one of the top officials in the Ministry of Finance. This official later supported the extension of gender work to other parts of the Ministry.

However, the average finance ministry usually views gender as peripheral to its work. Changing this mindset requires both political will and carefully crafted methods to create coopera-tion among finance officials. Some of the barriers to engender-ing the work of finance ministries include:

The success of a GRB initiative in effecting a change in government budget policy or allocations will depend on the degree of political support that it can attract from the highest levels of government ...

... NWMs are often handicapped by their small size, relative newness, poor access to human, technical and budgetary resources, lack of confidence in economics and relatively low position in the hierarchy of ministries.

- The Ministry usually does not have a clear understanding of how gender relates to its role.

- The Ministry's institutional power means that government agencies responsible for gender issues usually have little influence over it.

- Women's organisations tend to have limited knowledge and capacity to engage effectively in macroeconomic policy debates. Many are wary of working with numbers.

- The subject matter of finance ministries – macroeconomic aggregates and monetised variables rather than people – encourages the people who work there to become distanced from the impact of their work on people in the society.

The Women's/Gender Ministry

It is often difficult, even in inside-government initiatives, to decide on the specific role of the Women's/Gender Ministry – or national women's machinery – in gender budget work. On the one hand, finance ministries usually lack skills and interest in gender. On the other hand, the Women's/Gender Ministry usually lacks the technical skills and other resources necessary to lead gender budget work. In addition, allocating the lead role to the Finance Ministry is in line with the gender mainstreaming approach. This sees the NWM as providing support to other ministries, but locates gender-related initiatives firmly inside the ministries that have the responsibility for a particular function, in this case the budget.

One difficulty is that Finance Ministries and Women's/Gender Ministries usually have no tradition of working together. Another is that NWMs are often handicapped by their small size, relative newness, poor access to human, technical and budgetary resources, lack of confidence in economics and relatively low position in the hierarchy of ministries. Although theoretically their role is to provide advice or vet the work of other ministries, they often lack the institutional authority to do so effectively. As a result, in many countries the NWMs have played a minimal role in GRB initiatives.

On the other hand, the involvement of the NWM facilitates civil society engagement in the gender budget initiative as, in many countries, they are one of the government agencies most familiar with working with NGOs and other civil society groups.

In Australia, the women's budget initiatives were firmly located within the NWM, in the form of offices on the status of women. These offices coordinated the women's budget work and produced the publications that were tabled on budget day. The actual reporting on each sector agency's work was produced by officials of the agency concerned. However, the offices on the status of women provided guidance and co-ordination. In Rwanda, the Finance and Gender Ministries have together led the gender budget initiative. The good co-operation between them has been facilitated by the presence in the Gender Ministry of a long-term advisor with strong skills in economics.

Box 18: National Women's Machineries

National women's machineries (NWMs) were set up in response to the UN Decade for Women (1975–1985), the Convention on the Elimination of All Forms of Discrimination against Women (CEDAW) and the Nairobi Forward-Looking Strategies. The NWM is the body or system of bodies recognised by the government as responsible for spear-heading the promotion of the status of women, with a mandate to respond to women's/gender issues and concerns.

There are significant differences in the status, structure and functioning of NWMs in different countries. Some take the form of a ministry or department responsible for gender or women's affairs with their own minister. Some are located in the office of the Head of Government. Others are small units in diverse ministries or departments such as employment, health or community development. Many face severe financial, human and technical resource constraints. In general, NWMs experience marginalisation, which has a negative impact on their status in government and the wider society, and on their ability to influence government policy and access resources.

Adapted from Taylor, 1999

Sector ministries play a central role in GRBs. It is here that budgets are allocated to deliver goods and services. This is therefore where budgets must be transformed to provide for gender-responsive activities and programmes.

The Commonwealth Ministers Responsible for Women's Affairs played a crucial role in gaining the support of ministries of finance to implement GRBs.

Sector ministries

Sector ministries play a central role in GRBs. It is here that budgets are allocated to deliver goods and services. This is, therefore, where budgets must be transformed to provide for gender-responsive activities and programmes.

Within the sector ministries there are variations in terms of who is responsible for budgets. There can also be differences between who has responsibility in terms of: (a) compiling figures (budget officers); (b) developing programmes (planning officers); and (c) making decisions (accounting officers). In general, GRB initiatives have mainly involved middle-level technicians such as planners and budget officials. These officials regularly report that, while they fully appreciate the value of a GRB, the interventions need to gain the support of more senior officials because they make the real decisions.

On the one hand, this argument almost certainly reflects an effort to pass the buck. On the other, it is invariably true that decision-making takes place in a number of different places. The daunting message for gender budget work is the need to target all these different groups in terms of their roles. It may be more helpful to say that the top managers need to understand the importance of supporting GRBs, while the technicians need to understand how to do them.

Further complicating the issue are internal government tensions. The growing powers of the Ministry of Finance can lead to resistance from sectoral ministries, which see it as always imposing restrictions and controls. In Tanzania, for example, the sectoral officials in agencies that had not been specified as 'priorities' under the PRSP were unhappy about having to draw up detailed budgets. They felt these were futile because of the cash budgeting system imposed by the Ministry of Finance and Central Bank under the supervision of the IMF. This system is used in a range of countries in addition to Tanzania and means that the government only releases each month as much money as it has received in revenue. When revenue is less than expected – either because of donor delays or for other reasons – the Treasury attempts to give the priority agencies their full budgets by making cuts in the planned allocations for the non-priority agencies.

Legislatures

Many GRB initiatives target legislators. In some initiatives, legislators have played a leading role. Strategies include: (a) lobbying and training, particularly for women members; (b) presentations at legislative budget hearings; and (c) preparing fact sheets for use by legislators. These strategies might seem to tackle the pinnacle of budget decision-making power. However, as suggested in the previous section, many legislatures lack significant powers to change expenditures and revenues. In addition, even where there are women legislators, they will not necessarily openly support a GRB initiative. Where women legislators feel that their position depends on their political affiliation, they may be loath to be part of an initiative that is seen to be criticising government.

Despite the limitations, however, legislators can play a key role in GRBs, especially in outside-government initiatives. When civil society groups are leading gender budget work, legislators can provide:

- access to information;

- focus in terms of key issues; and

- greater legitimacy in political and other influential spheres.

... legislators can play a key role in GRBs, especially in outside-government initiatives.

Box 19: **Entry Points for Working with Legislators**

Identify legislative 'champions'. Legislative interventions in GRB initiatives work best when they are driven by people committed to the concerns raised by gender budget work. This has been the case in the Philippines, South Africa and Uganda. In most countries there is a tendency for women to lead on gender issues. However, the participation of male legislators avoids the marginalisation of GRBs as 'women's work'. Involvement of men is particularly important in legislatures where there are very few women.

Box 19 (*continued*)

Build a meaningful partnership. Legislators are more likely to support gender budget work if they receive support from those involved in GRB initiatives. This might include:

a) helping legislators understand the budget process and their role in it. Members of legislatures usually have diverse backgrounds (e.g. as teachers, doctors or community workers). Even where there are educational qualifications for standing for parliament, many legislators will be unfamiliar with the budget process, have limited understanding of economics and finance, and thus be wary of engagement;

b) sharing technical knowledge and other insights with legislators so that they can participate more meaningfully in the budget process. Some parliaments are fortunate in having legislative research units, but many do not have such units, or have small, overworked ones.

Support the work of legislative committees. In most countries different committees of the legislature have specific roles in the budget process. Usually, the Finance/Budget or Estimates Committee takes overall responsibility for parliament's role. However, there are usually also sectoral committees that discuss and comment on the ministries that fall within their ambit.

Other relevant committees for legislative influence include the Public Accounts Committee and Status of Women Committee. The former is responsible for scrutiny of past expenditure, which it does on the basis of reports from the Office of the Auditor-General. The Status of Women Committee, where it exists, forms part of the NWM in that its role is to check that gender is mainstreamed in all parliament's work. There can be natural alliances between the OAG, the Public Accounts Committee and gender budget groups in monitoring and reporting on the budget. Where Status of Women Committees exist, the results of gender budget analyses can be an important resource for the Committee's members in ensuring that women's interests are equally and equitably reflected in the budget.

Without such entry-points to government, outputs of outside government initiatives can be easily overlooked by those involved in budget decision-making, or used only among a limited group of gender activists. Collaboration with legislators can produce a win–win situation as civil society groups can provide the technical expertise and time necessary to collect information, undertake the research and produce the analysis, which is then used by legislators (see box 19).

The South Africa's Women's Budget Initiative is a classic example of a legislature-civil society alliance. The formation of the alliance was facilitated by the large increase in the number of women parliamentarians in the 1994 elections and the fact that many of these women were part of the broad women's movement in the country. Women in strategic positions in relation to the budget, such as on the Finance Committee, were particularly keen to have an initiative that would support them in their new roles.

In Uganda, the NGO that coordinates the gender budget initiative was established by women parliamentarians and worked closely with the women's caucus in parliament. Again, the fact that 30 per cent of parliamentarians were women provided a solid base of support. In the Philippines, it was a senator who in 1995 fought for and won the legislation providing that 5 per cent of every agency's budget should be set aside for gender. This provision, which is known as the Gender and Development Budget, was later extended to all local government agencies.

Collaboration with legislators can produce a win–win situation as civil society groups can provide the technical expertise and time necessary to collect information, undertake the research and produce the analysis, which is then used by legislators.

Office of the Auditor-General

The Office of the Auditor-General plays a lead role in monitoring the implementation of the budget. To date, gender budget work has not taken advantage of this potential route for participating in the tracking of government expenditure. Some of the reasons for this are that:

a) The OAG usually maintains a low profile outside the legislative process, leaving it to legislators to make public statements on any financial wrongdoing.

b) Legislators, with whom budget groups would usually collaborate, have little incentive to pay much attention to

The Office of the Auditor-General plays a lead role in monitoring the implementation of the budget. To date, gender budget work has not taken advantage of this potential route for participating in the tracking of government expenditure.

expenditure in past years due to their often limited legislative budget power.

c) The audit function is often delayed, with reports produced two or more years after the financial year ends. At that stage, it seems more sensible for budget groups to focus their limited resources and the public interest on current budgets.

For gender budget groups interested in monitoring government expenditure, there are spaces opening up for civil society participation in auditing of the budget. One such initiative is public/budget expenditure tracking. This usually involves government agencies collecting and making available data on their service provision. These data allow for detection of delayed or partial transfers of funds between agencies, deficiencies of the frontline service providers, and possible wastage and corruption. If data are disaggregated, they can also allow for detection of inequity in terms of beneficiaries of services. To date, these exercises have tended to focus on the health and education sectors.

Civil society groups can also attempt to follow the flow of funds for specific government projects. Examples of civil society involvement in budget expenditure tracking include the Government Watch initiative of the Philippine Governance Forum, and the Mazdoor Kisaan Shakti Sangathan in India. Government Watch examined expenditures for specific projects in education, health and public works while MKSS sought to expose corruption in local government (see box 17). The Zimbabwe Women's Resource Centre and Network (ZWRCN) has a project to track allocations of the country's AIDS levy. In undertaking the tracking, ZWRCN is particularly interested in whether the levy is being used to address gender issues, including the burden of home-based care.

Individuals

Individuals in government have been key to ensuring the achievements of the more successful initiatives. As noted above, having a champion is particularly important in the early years, when people have to be convinced of the need to put energy into what seems a difficult and strange area of intervention.

However, it is important to institutionalise the initiatives so that they become part of the everyday function of government officials. If this does not happen, there is a danger that gender-responsive budgeting will fall away when there is a shift in political power.

External agencies

It should be an underlying principle of gender budget work that it is 'owned' by national stakeholders, as the work is essentially about what is done with citizens' money. Nonetheless, external agencies can play a positive role in gender budget work at the country level. The Commonwealth Secretariat was one of the first external agencies to get involved in this area of work. Through the years, the Secretariat has provided support to country initiatives both through technical assistance and through encouraging an enabling environment for this work to take root. It has produced tools, methodology and capacity-building materials; contributed to international advocacy; and encouraged collaboration between agencies interested in supporting work in this area. The tools, for example, include several designed by Diane Elson that could be used for gender-sensitive analysis of budgets (see Elson, 2002a). The challenge to external agencies is to ensure that they maintain a supportive rather than a dominant role in the implementation of gender budget work.

In addition to multilateral and bilateral official aid agencies,

... external agencies can play a positive role in gender budget work at the country level.

Literacy class for rural women.

INTERNATIONAL LABOUR ORGANIZATION/
J. MAILLARD

international NGOs and foundations have provided both financial and other support to gender budget work. In general, the official aid agencies tend to favour support for government initiatives, while the international NGOs and foundations are more likely to fund exercises that focus on civil society. In some countries, official donors are contractually constrained in terms of whom they can support. For example, some country agreements state that the donor agency needs permission from the government before it gives money to NGOs.

> ### *Box 20:* External Agencies Involved in Gender-responsive Budgets
>
> Gender budget work in developing countries has been supported by a number of external agencies, including the Asian Development Bank (ADB), Asia Foundation, Charles Stewart Mott Foundation, Commonwealth Secretariat, European Commission, Ford Foundation, German Technical Cooperation Agency (GTZ), International Development Research Centre (IDRC), Oxfam Canada, Swedish International Development Cooperation Agency (Sida), Swiss Agency for Development and Cooperation, UK Department for International Development (DfID), the Governments of Denmark, Netherlands and Norway, the United Nations Development Programme (UNDP), the United Nations Development Fund for Women (UNIFEM) and the World Bank Institute. In addition, the World Bank has promoted the idea of GRB analysis in its gender publications. The IMF has also recently produced a Working Paper on the topic (Sarraf, 2003). This looks, in particular, at how new ways of budgeting such as programme performance budgets "can help promote gender equality ... at any level of available funding".
>
> Source: Budlender *et al.*, 2002

External support has its drawbacks. These fall under three main headings: (1) financial dependency; (2) the methods used; and (3) the use of consultants.

1. Financial dependency

Financial dependency poses dangers to programme sustainability. However, money is usually necessary if the exercises are to be anything beyond small, one-off interventions. Ironically, developed country initiatives are disadvantaged in this respect as there are far fewer donors active in these countries. But the very extensive role of donors in developing countries also introduces challenges for the budget initiatives. One of these is resistance among both government and non-government players to donor-driven initiatives. For many potential supporters of gender budget work, the involvement of the World Bank could discourage participation because of their perception of the nature of past Bank activities.

2. The methods used

The methods commonly adopted in donor-funded initiatives can also be a challenge. For example, workshops are one of the most popular activities. One reason is that this activity is easily measurable in terms of logical framework planning. Workshops are clearly valid in that they are a good way of spreading new ideas to a group of people. They are particularly useful in the case of gender budget work, where one of the important first steps is often basic consciousness-raising around gender issues. However, in many countries the persistence of 'sitting allowances', or other payments to participants, raises questions about the motives of those attending the workshop. Particularly where civil servants earn tiny salaries, participating in workshops can be an end in itself.

There are also questions as to the difference workshops make in relation to what people do in their work. Changing mindsets is the first step, but the ultimate objective is to change what officials do so that things are better for citizens. If the initiative is to have an impact on the lives of those whom it professes to target, initiatives must extend beyond raising awareness to empowering officials with concrete tools and practical support.

Some of the GRB training exercises have attempted to respond to the concern around 'output' by requiring that there be a concrete 'product', in the form of a report on findings by the different sectors participating and an action plan. Where

If the initiative is to have an impact on the lives of those whom it professes to target, initiatives must extend beyond raising awareness to empowering officials with concrete tools and practical support.

the workshop participants are government officials, this can elicit questions about payment for work that they perceive to be additional to their ordinary workload. The danger of providing payment is that this could reinforce the perception that gender is something 'extra' rather than something that should be mainstreamed in everyday work.

3. The use of consultants

Using consultants can also be a problem. Most bilateral and multilateral funding comes with the expectation that there will be external 'expert' technical assistance in addition to the funds. In some cases there is the additional expectation that the experts will come from the funding country. Goetz notes that development agencies generally tend to value information from Western feminists and researchers more than that of women in developing countries. She compares this privileging of certain voices to the privileging of economists and economics over development practitioners and theorists (Goetz, 1994:28). Both of these forms of privilege are important to remember in GRB work.

The potential for problems is heightened by differences in terms of money and power. On the financial side, the external expert is usually paid substantially more than the local counterpart, if there is one. In terms of power, the external expert will often have divided loyalties, particularly if the employing agency is the funder. Even if the government or local partner is the employing agency, the influence of the funder may be evident behind the scenes.

There is also the issue of the capacity of the consultant. Evaluating expertise in an area like gender budget work is extremely difficult. The work is still largely experimental, so there are no simple rules and tools to pass on. Budget work is also a very 'national' issue. While there are many similarities in the way budgets are prepared across countries, and multilateral and bilateral agencies have attempted to standardise approaches, there are still important differences even in the basic format. There are other differences in terms of both theoretical and actual processes of budget making. Added to that are the political considerations.

An experienced 'expert' might know some of the questions

to ask, but could also be blinkered because of exposure to a limited number of other situations. Admittedly, in many countries few gender activists have knowledge about budget matters. On the other hand, they do have an understanding of the gender and political situation in the country. How to best bring these different knowledge bases and experiences together is not a simple issue.

Determining the Focus of the Initiative

GRB initiatives serve different purposes for different players. For governments, gender budgets are used: (a) as an internal management tool to increase budgetary performance; (b) for accountability purposes to the legislature, women and the public at large; and (c) for monitoring and reporting on action taken against international commitments. Civil society and the legislature use gender budgets as a means to hold government to account.

Some actors will undertake gender budget initiatives as a more or less stand-alone activity with its own objectives. Others – and particularly civil society groups already engaged in advocacy – will want to use the gender budget approach to elaborate and strengthen their non-budget advocacy. For all actors, gender budgets are a tool rather than an end in themselves – a tool to advance a particular policy advocacy, to increase budget accountability and to enhance gender equality in a particular country. The objectives underpinning the GRB initiative will determine its focus.

One possible initial strategy is to select a limited number of sectors (government portfolios). The selection of the sectors requires some thought. It is readily accepted that 'social' portfolios such as education, health and welfare have significant gender implications. However, other areas such as legal affairs, industry, agriculture, land and water have considerable impacts on gender. Many developing countries choose to start with education and health because these were subjected to brutal cuts during structural adjustment programmes. Many choose agriculture as one of the early sectors because of its importance in terms of women's economic engagement. The Korean NGO WomenLink began by studying the budgets allocated for

For all actors, gender budgets are a tool rather than an end in themselves – a tool to advance a particular policy advocacy, to increase budget accountability and to enhance gender equality in a particular country.

Organisations concerned with specific gender issues may choose to focus on a single issue rather than on the budget of a particular ministry or other agency. In some cases, this approach will entail analysis of parts of a range of different budgets.

women-related policies as the country had recently established new laws, institutions and policies in respect of women.

The South African Women's Budget Initiative (WBI) is one of the few to have covered all sectors of government. The Initiative wanted to do a comprehensive analysis to prove that gender could be found in all portfolios. However, as in other countries, the WBI began with a pilot that focused on only six sectors so as to be able to test and develop its method. In choosing the first six sectors, the initiators ensured that the selection included both economic and social sectors, so as to undermine perceptions that gender is only relevant in the latter. In the second year, the WBI looked at three ministries from the protective sphere – justice, prisons and police.

Organisations concerned with specific gender issues may choose to focus on a single issue rather than on the budget of a particular ministry or other agency. In some cases, this approach will entail analysis of parts of a range of different budgets. An example of the approach again comes from South Africa, where the NGO Gender Advocacy Programme commissioned another NGO to conduct analysis into the resources allocated for implementing the Domestic Violence Act. The analysis covered both national and provincial governments, and sectors such as justice, prisons, police, health and welfare. The research was used in subsequent advocacy by the Gender Advocacy Programme and others for improved implementation of the Act. Subsequently, another South African NGO took the focus on gender violence and budgets further (see box 21).

Working at the Sub-national Level

Bolivia, Chile, Mexico, Peru, the Philippines, South Africa, Tanzania and Uganda are among the countries that have initiated gender budget work at the sub-national level. Projects planned for the future suggest that there will be more work at this level in the coming years.

Local level interventions are appropriate given that many countries – often under pressure from multilateral and bilateral institutions – are increasingly decentralising functions and budgets. Pragmatically, then, it makes sense to follow the

Box 21: Case Study: Focusing on Gender Violence and Budgets (South Africa)

The Centre for the Study of Violence and Reconciliation (CSVR) in South Africa had been involved for many years in the area of gender violence and had provided training for staff of the specialist Family Violence, Child Protection and Sexual Offences (FCS) units, among others. Through this experience, CSVR recognised that training alone would not solve the problems. In particular, adequate financial resources were needed to ensure that there were staff, skills and all the other things in place necessary to provide services effectively and compassionately.

CSVR's research and advocacy focused on three aspects of budgets for gender violence:

1. Government support for NGOs providing services to women experiencing gender-based violence.
CSVR sent out a survey to the nearly 200 organisations in the country that they knew were providing services for women who had experienced gender-based violence. About three-quarters responded, and analysis of the returns revealed how much (or how little) different government departments were assisting these organisations. CSVR followed up on the survey with training and a manual for organisations that could help them lobby for further support from government.

2. National and provincial budgetary allocations for developing and implementing policies.
This aspect was more difficult because some departments were slow to provide information, despite a letter from a parliamentary committee supporting the research. Another challenge was that government departments often do not provide enough detail and disaggregation to show how much money goes for fighting gender violence. However, CSVR succeeded in painting a fairly detailed picture showing some gaps between policy and budgets.

A shift of focus to the sub-national level must be based on an understanding of both the potential advantages and disadvantages of decentralisation, and how this should affect the focus and scope of the work.

Box 21 (*continued*)

3. Estimates of the costs of violence against women to the state, society and individuals.
CSVR interviewed a diverse set of women to illustrate the very different impact that violence might have on the budgets of women, depending on whether they were poor or rich, rural or urban, old or young, or disabled or able-bodied.

money and decision-making power. So in Mexico, for example, Fundar and Equidad de Genero focus on the sub-national level, motivated by the shift in budget responsibility to states and municipalities, particularly in social spending. They note that the decentralisation process has made "controversial local budget decisions the centre of publicised political debates for the first time ever" (Fundar and Equidad de Genero, 1999:2).

A shift of focus to the sub-national level must be based on an understanding of both the potential advantages and disadvantages of decentralisation, and how this should affect the focus and scope of the work. There may be a need to question decentralisation trends where, for example, this is accompanied by increasing inequality between the decentralised units or where functions are delegated, but money is not. Too often decentralisation can mean that the state is absolving itself of responsibilities, but attempting to do so in a way that is less visible. Often decentralisation will be justified by arguments that this promotes local 'ownership' and increases accountability, whereas in fact local areas are simply being left to rely on their own meagre resources. So, for example, decentralisation is often accompanied by an increase in user fees for services. All of these aspects of decentralisation have gender implications. A local level focus needs to look both at what is happening in individual locations and at inter-governmental fiscal relations as a whole. The Third Women's Budget in South Africa provides one example of the latter aspect (De Bruyn and Budlender, 1998).

In Uganda, the Forum for Women in Democracy argues that local level interventions are sensible in that poor women are unlikely, due to resource limitations, to be able to exert influence outside this sphere. Interventions at this level may not, however, be easy. In many countries, traditional and potentially oppressive gender relations will often be more entrenched at local levels, while national leaders tend to be more aware of gender equity issues. The more blatant power relations – both in terms of gender and other factors – are directly reflected in local budgets in some countries. In the Philippines, for example, the Local Government Units' budgets usually contain a sizeable mayoral allocation over which the mayor has virtually complete discretion.

Where local government bodies are relatively small, the relationships between the key actors are often more direct and personal. The nature of these relationships needs to be taken into account in devising strategies. FOWODE's local initiative has engaged directly with the relationship issue by involving a wider range of players than at national level. So, for example, their first workshop brought together the MPs elected in the districts, local councillors, local government officials and NGOs. One of the most heated debates during the training occurred when councillors' allowances were discussed.

Given the fluidity and changes in decentralised structures occurring in many countries, local level GRB initiatives that are directed at civil society or public representatives need to be clear about the functions of different levels of government. This is important for advocacy purposes to prevent effort and resources being spent in lobbying those who have no power to address a particular problem. The differences across countries in the distribution of functions at different levels require that special attention be paid to this when engaging in cross-country work.

Accessing Resources

The UNIFEM/Commonwealth Secretariat/International Development Resource Centre (IDRC) GRB website (*www. gender-budgets.org*) contains a collection of background documents, tools and training materials and other useful reference materials. These include:

Gender Budget Initiatives: Strategies, Concepts and Experiences (UNIFEM, 2002)

Gender Budgets Make Cents (Budlender *et al.*, 2002)
Gender Budgets Make More Cents (Budlender and Hewitt, 2002)
The Political Economy of Women's Budgets in the South (Budlender, 2000)

The website is being redesigned to include detailed country information and to allow practitioners to post details on their programmes directly on the site. IDRC/UNIFEM/Commonwealth hope that this will encourage greater sharing of information between practitioners and across countries.

BRIDGE has also produced a useful collection of resources in their *Cutting-Edge Pack on Gender and Budgets* (see *www.ids.ac.uk/bridge*). It includes case studies from across the globe; information on tools, guidelines and training materials and popular education materials; Internet-based resources; and contact details for networking, information exchange and possible programme support. BRIDGE has also produced the very helpful *Glossary on Macroeconomics from a Gender Perspective* (Alexander with Baden, 2000).

In addition, the section below on 'Analysing the situation of women, men, girls and boys' contains several suggestions for accessing national and international sources of gender-specific information and data. A number of other resources can be found in the bibliography.

4. Applying the Analytical Framework

There are two basic frameworks that, with variations, have served as the basis of many exercises to date. These are the Australian (Sharp) three-way categorisation of expenditure and the South African five-step approach mentioned at the beginning of Part 1. These two methods can be reconciled into a common analytical framework which can be used as the basis for either analysis of existing budgets or reporting by sector ministries. For example, a government initiative might take a particular department or ministry, look at its programmes and sub-programmes – distinguishing between the three categories – and analyse and report on each in terms of the five steps. This is more or less what the standard Australian gender budget format did. A civil society initiative, on the other hand, would not necessarily start with a government unit and its budget. Instead, it might look at a particular gender issue, go through the five steps and look at which programmes and sub-programmes – possibly from a range of ministries – address the gender issue, and which do so in terms of each of the three categories.

The Three-way Categorisation

This distinguishes between:

1. Gender-specific expenditure;

2. Equal opportunity expenditure for civil servants; and

3. General expenditure (the rest) considered in terms of its gendered impact.

This classification has proved useful in pointing out that a focus on the limited funds usually allocated to category (1) misses the point of the exercise. It has also proved useful when working with government officials in highlighting the need to move from a focus on opportunities for women civil servants (category 2) to the impact of government expenditure generally on the public (category 3).

One weakness of this framework, however, is the potential confusion between women and gender. The Australian exercise was framed in terms of 'women' rather than 'gender', and many users today still tend to conflate the two concepts. This can be misleading when conducting analysis. In particular, expenditures that are targeted at women may not necessarily advance gender equity. For example, family planning programmes that focus only on population control through control of women's bodies would usually not be regarded as gender-sensitive.

1. Gender-specific expenditure allocations

This involves an assessment of the specifically gender-targeted allocations by:

- Identifying the aim of the listed programme or project, including the problem to be addressed (steps 1 and 2 of the five-step approach, see below);

- Identifying the activities planned to implement the programme or project (step 2);

- Quantifying the allocation of resources (step 3);

- Determining output indicators (e.g. the number of women or men beneficiaries) (step 4);

- Determining impact or outcome indicators, to measure changes in the situation of women, men, girls and boys (step 5);

- Noting changes planned in the coming year, to assess whether the budget is becoming more or less gender-responsive.

2. Equal employment opportunities in the public sector

The equal opportunity issues in public sector employment are analysed by:

- Describing employment patterns within particular sector(s) or the public sector as a whole;

- Disaggregating by sex, levels of employment (grades), forms of employment (full or part-time, permanent or temporary), salaries and benefits. Other disaggregations such as race and disability could also be included;

- Identifying any special initiatives to promote equal employment opportunities – amounts spent and numbers reached (e.g. women in management training or gender training for officials);

- Determining the number of women and men in positions with a gender focus or specialisation (e.g. gender focal points; police, medical and welfare officials dealing with rape and domestic violence; or men in positions dealing with men and gender violence);

- Disaggregating by sex the membership of boards and committees established under the sector(s) (distinguishing between paid and unpaid appointments and levels of remuneration);

- Describing any changes planned in the coming year.

In gender budget work, gender issues in public sector employment can be thought about in two ways. Firstly, salaries account for a large proportion of most government budgets. Public service employment patterns show who benefits directly from these salaries. The patterns thus reflect (or not) principles of equal employment opportunities between men and women and between groups of men and women. Secondly, the presence of women or men in particular positions can affect the gender-responsiveness of decision-making and delivery of services.

3. General expenditure allocations

General or mainstream budget allocations can be analysed in a manner similar to gender-specific allocations. However, because there are usually many programmes and projects within any given sector, choices have to be made as to which to focus on. Useful criteria in making these choices are the size (in terms of budget) of different programmes, and the importance in gender terms of the issues they are addressing.

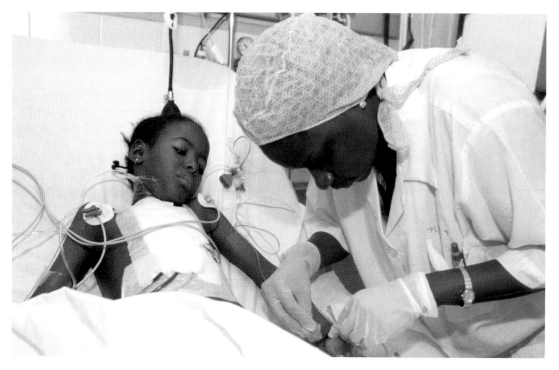

Nurse in intensive care unit.
INTERNATIONAL LABOUR ORGANIZATION/
P. DELOCHE

The Five-step Approach

The five-steps are:

1. Analysing the situation of women, men, girls and boys;

2. Assessing the gender-responsiveness of policies;

3. Assessing budget allocations;

4. Monitoring spending and service delivery;

5. Assessing outcomes.

This framework has been used either implicitly or explicitly for outside-government initiatives such as those in the Philippines, South Africa, Tanzania and Uganda. It is also useful for inside-government initiatives in countries that are implementing programme or performance budgeting as the latter has a similar approach, minus the disaggregation introduced by a GRB framework. In Rwanda, for example, a 'Gender Annex' to the 2003 budget analysed the gender dimensions, outputs, activities and indicators of programmes in the various ministries. Table 1 is an abridged version of a page from the Ministry of Health.

Table 1: An Example of Gender Analysis in the 2003 Budget of Rwanda

Ministry of Health	Gender Dimensions	Outputs	Activities	Indicators
Fight against HIV/AIDS	• Due to biological reasons, women and girls are more vulnerable to HIV/AIDS than men. • Furthermore, inmost cases, pregnant women suffering from AIDS transmit the virus to their babies. • Current gender relations do not give women and girls a great deal of power to protect themselves against unsafe sexual relations. • Sexual violence constantly exerted on little girls exposes the latter to a serious risk of infection.	1. The vertical transmission programme is integrated in 10 health facilities; 2. 20 VCT sites were open by December 2003; 3. Support for HIV/AIDS research; 4. A survey of syphilis cases among pregnant women is conducted every year; 5. A disaggregated national survey on HIV-positive cases linked to HIV/AIDS is undertaken annually; 6. The Laboratory to complete an analysis of the HIV molecular biology, each year.	• The HIV/AIDS prevention programme that targets specifically men, women, girls and boys. • Undertake an HIV prevalence study at national level. • Promote access to female and male condoms. • Undertake a syphilis prevalence study. • Awareness programmes for people at risk, such as prostitutes, lorry drivers, military men, etc. • Make treatment available to men and women. • Take the necessary measures to avoid vertical transmission of HIV.	• Percentage of infected women and girls, men and boys. • Number and percentage of HIV positive women/girls and men/boys who have access to treatment. • Number of women/girls and men/boys specifically targeted by HIV/AIDS prevention awareness programmes. • Availability and accessibility (affordable price) of the female condom.

In practice, the main weakness in the use of this approach has been a limited ability to move beyond the second step. Generally, the researchers involved are practised in describing the situation and discussing policy, but the sections on the budget are brief and often weak. The blame does not always lie with the researchers. Often the necessary data are simply not available. However, in many cases the facts are there for those who look. While many complain that budgets tell very little, even the simplest tables sometimes expose serious imbalances. The documents that accompany the budget figures can also be revealing.

In all countries, gender disadvantage coexists with other forms of disadvantage. For example, in most countries rural people will be disadvantaged compared to urban, and poor compared to rich.

1. Analysing the situation of women, men, girls and boys

One of the outcomes of gender budget work was to uncover the scarcity of gender-disaggregated data on the comparative situation of women and men, girls and boys in relation to particular sectors. This situation severely constrains the ability of those involved to identify and respond to situations of gender disadvantage. Regarding the gender debate in the Caribbean, for example, a country coordinator of a GRB initiative noted that "officials in government are not always aware enough of the [gender] issues nor seized with the empirical data surrounding the subject to make an informed comment or contribute to the process [of addressing gender concerns]. This notwithstanding, comments abound and there is a massive debate" (Dalrymple, 2000).

In all countries, gender disadvantage coexists with other forms of disadvantage. For example, in most countries rural people will be disadvantaged compared to urban, and poor compared to rich. There are usually additional country-specific disadvantages in terms of race, ethnicity, age and so on. These other axes of disadvantage need to be considered when collecting information to assess the gender situation, as there are likely to be significant differences between women and girls from different sub-groups, as there are between men and boys from different sub-groups.

Gathering the information needed to analyse the situation of women, men, girls and boys (and their different sub-groups) can be done through a combination of national (local) and international sources that include international compendiums, cross-country statistical data, national development plans, government policy documents, official government statistics, administrative data and independent research. Because of the history of gender bias against females, most documents that analyse the gender situation concentrate their findings on the status of women and girls.

Box 22: Recommendations for Basic Gender-disaggregated Data

The Swedish Statistics Agency, in its publication *Engendering Statistics: A Tool For Change*, suggests that basic sex-disaggregated information should be available in order to measure the underlying causes of gender problems and the gender consequences and effects. The list below is an adaptation of their recommendations, which may be useful indicators for gender budget work.

Sex segregation in education:
- Primary level enrolment ratios;
- Basic level enrolment ratios;
- Secondary level enrolment ratios;
- Tertiary level enrolment ratios;
- Adult education enrolment ratios;
- Secondary and tertiary level enrolment by field of study;
- Levels of education attained by adult population (18 years and over);
- Urban/rural differences in primary, secondary and tertiary level enrolment;
- Dropout, absenteeism and repetition rates in schools.

Unequal sharing of responsibilities within the family:
- Time spent in paid and unpaid work by marital status, age, and number and age of children;
- Employed population by marital status, age, and number and age of children;
- Time spent by children working in the household and/or in subsistence agriculture.

Women's reproductive role:
- Total fertility rate;
- Fertility rate by age, marital status and urban/rural location;
- Economically/not economically active population by marital status and number of children.

> **Box 22** (*continued*)
>
> *Women's access to shelter:*
> * Restrictions on property/home ownership;
> * Headship of household by marital status;
> * Legal ownership or joint ownership by marital status;
> * Residence with extended family or other relations by marital status.
>
> *Source:* Hedman *et al.*, 1996: 50–53

In-country sources of gender-specific information and data

These include:

* census data;
* household surveys;
* national statistics service;
* national women's machinery (NWM);
* sectoral agencies for administrative data;
* university departments, research institutes and libraries;
* women's organisations and other civil society organisations (CSOs);
* think tanks and independent research institutes.

The South African Constitution of 1995 places the same emphasis on equality in terms of sex and gender as it places on racial equality. The need to measure race explicitly thus went alongside the recognition of the importance of gender-disaggregation of all statistics and indicators. The importance of disaggregation was written into law in 1999 when the parliamentary Committee on the Quality of Life and Status of Women proposed an amendment to the new Statistics Act (No 6 of 1999). Clause 3(2)(g) states that all official statistics must be "sensitive to distribution by gender, disability, region and similar socio-economic features".

The Philippines Women in Development and Nation-Building Act is the legislation that introduced the 5 per cent GAD Budget described above. This same Act mandates government to produce gender-disaggregated data.

International sources of on-line gender-specific information

These include:

GenderStats: a database of gender statistics developed by the World Bank (http://genderstats.worldbank.org). This site provides country-specific information in the following categories: basic demographic data; population dynamics; labour force structure; education; health; and country policy and institutional assessment (CPIA) indicators. International comparisons are also included on women in development, education outcomes and reproductive health. The World Bank is planning to introduce country gender assessments (CGAs) as part of a new strategy for mainstreaming gender-responsive actions into its development assistance work (see box 23).

United Nations Statistics Division (http://unstats.un.org/unsd). This division compiles statistics from many international sources. It also provides specifications of the best methods of compiling information so that data from different sources can be readily compared. On-line access is available to global data, such as the Millennium Country Profiles, which list 48 social and economic indicators by country and year since 1985; a database of social indicators, which monitors the results of recent major United Nations conferences on children, population and development, social development and women; and the publication *The World's Women 2000: Trends and Statistics.* The latter is a five-yearly statistical source-book analysing how women compare to men worldwide in the areas of families, health, education, work, population, human rights and politics.

United Nations Economic Commission for Europe (UNECE): Gender Statistics Website for Europe and North America (http://www.unece.org/stats/gender). This gender statistics site aims to bring together both gender statistics and policies in order to monitor the situation of women and men in all UNECE member countries and evaluate the effectiveness of policies. The site also has a section that provides general information on producing, presenting and disseminating gender statistics, as well as international standards and guidelines. (The UN Economic Commission for Africa is currently coordinating an African Gender and Development Index exercise.

By the end of the pilot phase – the end of 2003 – this should produce a range of statistics on the situation of women and men in 13 African countries.)

Box 23: **The World Bank's Country Gender Assessments**

A country gender assessment normally includes:

- A profile of:
  a) The different socio-economic roles of males and females, including their participation in both the market and household economies;
  b) Gender disparities in access to, control over and use of assets and productive resources;
  c) Gender disparities in human development indicators;
  d) Inequalities between males and females in their ability to participate in development decision-making at the local and national levels;
  e) Laws, institutional frameworks, norms and other societal practices that lead (implicitly or explicitly) to gender discrimination and/or gender inequality;

- The country context, including the country's policies, priorities, legal and regulatory framework, and institutional arrangements for implementing its gender and development goals;

- A review of the gender dimensions of the Bank's portfolio of ongoing projects in the country;

- A set of suggested gender-responsive priority policy and operational interventions that are seen as important for poverty reduction and development effectiveness.

Source: World Bank, 2002

United Nations Human Development Report (http://hdr.undp.org/). The Human Development Report's primary purpose is to assess the state of human development across the globe and provide a critical analysis of a specific theme each year. It combines thematic policy analysis with detailed country data that focus on human well-being, not just economic trends. This annual report does not specifically focus on gender (except for the 1995 edition), but the site maintains a statistical database (current 2002 statistics) that provides gender-specific country data of interest for the calculation of the gender-related development index (GDI) and gender empowerment measure (GEM). The website thus includes data on education, health, income, decision-making and participation in economic and political life.

2. Assessing the gender-responsiveness of policies

The objective of this step is to assess whether a particular policy or programme is likely to increase gender inequalities described in the previous step, leave them the same or reduce them. Some countries have overall gender policies that state how they see the gender inequalities in the country and what they plan to do to address them. Some countries go further to develop sector-specific gender policies that perform a similar function for that specific sector. Whether or not there is a gender policy, it is also important to look at the general, mainstream policies both for the sector and for development as a whole. The mainstream policies must be examined for what they say, either implicitly or explicitly, about gender. They must also be looked at to see whether they contradict the gender policies in any way.

The following documents could be useful in identifying the gender-responsiveness of policy in a particular country:

- National development plan, poverty reduction strategy paper and similar documents;

- National women's/gender policy;

- National Action Plan on strategies to implement the Beijing Platform for Action (PFA);

- Reports under the Convention on the Elimination of All Forms of Discrimination against Women;

- Sectoral policies;

- Policy analyses conducted by academics and women's organisations;

Whether or not there is a gender policy, it is also important to look at the general, mainstream policies both for the sector and for development as a whole ... for what they say, either implicitly or explicitly, about gender.

- Policy analyses conducted by multilateral and bilateral development agencies.

A useful place to locate some of this information is the website of the United Nations Division for the Advancement of Women (UNDAW): Country Information (*http://www.un.org/womenwatch/daw/country*). The information contained on the site includes:

- National Action Plans called for by the Beijing PFA;

- Responses to the Secretary-General's Questionnaire to Governments on Implementation of the Beijing PFA;

- Country reports submitted under CEDAW.

The website also contains a table giving a complete listing of countries and their compliance with implementing the Beijing PFA and other international legal instruments on women.

Sometimes governments and particular sectors have not produced policy documents or strategic plans. In these cases, those doing gender budget work will have to deduce policies from budget statements or expenditure allocations. This is easier in countries that utilise programme or performance budgeting than in countries that have simple, accounting-type budget formats.

3. Assessing budget allocations

With the background of the situation and policy analyses, the focus of the third step shifts to the budget itself. The main aim in this step is to see whether the budget allocations are adequate to implement the gender-responsive policy identified in the second step. If the second step reveals that policy is gender-insensitive, or may even exacerbate gender inequality, the third step can be used to reveal the extent to which funds are being misallocated.

The main source for this information is the budget book itself. In some cases there are several different tabulations of the budget – for example, by function, accounting category and programme. Tabulations by programme are the most useful for gender budget analysis, especially if they contain information about objectives and indicators. In addition to the tabulations, governments often table documents that discuss the performance of the different ministries over the past year and plans for the coming year. These, together with the budget speech, assist in analysis of the budget figures.

The budgets that are tabled in parliament are often summary documents that do not provide as much information as desirable. With good contacts inside government, it may be possible to obtain more detailed budgets, such as the budget for a particular programme or sub-programme.

4. Monitoring spending and service delivery

The types of data needed for gender budget analysis can be divided into three broad categories:

i.   *Inputs* measure what is put into the process (e.g. the amount of money budgeted or the staff allocated for a particular programme or project);

ii. *Outputs* measure direct products of a particular programme or project (e.g. the number of beneficiaries receiving medical services or the number of clinics built);

iii. *Outcomes* measure the results of the policy or programme (e.g. increased health, educational levels and availability of time) (see step 5).

All three types of data are necessary. Where a country has adopted programme or performance budgeting, it will usually include some output measures in its budget document. However, these will probably not be disaggregated by gender or in any other way. Even where government does supply some output indicators, it is worthwhile to investigate whether other indicators are available (e.g. from administrative data).

Governments or outside-government analysts might also be interested in developing a number of cross-cutting indicators of the gender-responsiveness of budgets. The Commonwealth Secretariat GRB Initiative identified a number of possible indicators that could be used to prepare a GRB statement. They included:

• The share of total expenditure targeted to gender equality programmes;

It is also usually very difficult to attribute a given outcome to a particular, or single, policy or project. Ultimately, however, a policy or project must be judged on the basis of outcomes.

- Gender balance in public-sector employment (i.e. the number of women and men at different levels and in different jobs);

- The share of expenditure devoted to women's priority needs from public services;

- The share of expenditure devoted to the NWM and to the gender units within each ministry;

- The share of expenditure on income transfers devoted to women's priorities (e.g. child-support grants to care-givers of young children in poor households);

- Gender balance in business support, such as the subsidies, training or credit provided by the Ministry of Agriculture and the Ministry of Trade and Industry;

- Gender balance in public sector contracts awarded, including contracts to build houses or for public works;

- Gender balance in membership of government committees and other decision-making bodies and forums;

- Gender balance in government training programmes (Elson, 2002a).

5. Assessing outcomes

A given change in policy or in a project will affect inputs and outputs far more quickly than it affects outcomes. It is also usually very difficult to attribute a given outcome to a particular, or single, policy or project. Ultimately, however, a policy or project must be judged on the basis of outcomes.

In Malaysia, for example, although the country does not yet have a GRB, there is a well-developed programme performance budgeting system in place in respect of the operating budget. Every ministry reports according to this format each year on all the activities of every programme. The final two items of the format are 'indicator of impact' and 'programme evaluation plan'. The former requires that the ministry state what issues will be evaluated and the methodology. The latter requires the ministry to state when the last evaluation was done, when the next one will be done, and what the main criteria are that will be evaluated in the future reviews. It would be easy to incorporate gender issues into both these items. The Malaysian approach acknowledges that impact is not something that can be 'seen' on an annual basis. A system of evaluations that happen more than once a year ensures that impact is not forgotten.

In Tanzania, a different approach was suggested. This was that each year, together with the budget, the government should table a list of indicators showing overall progress in achieving gender equality. The proposed indicators were compiled by choosing one or two indicators for each of the articles of the Beijing PFA. Criteria in choosing the indicators were that the necessary data would be relatively easily available and able to be updated each year. One weakness of this approach is that it does not make a direct link between particular government programmes and particular indicators.

Analysing Revenue-raising Measures

As expenditure and revenue are opposite sides of the same budget coin, it is important to ensure that the revenue base is large enough to support expenditure for government programmes. UNIFEM, the Commonwealth Secretariat and the International Development Resource Centre have commissioned consultants to develop tools that can be used for gender-sensitive analysis of revenue. The five-step process described above in looking at expenditure could also be easily adapted to look at revenue (see box 24).

Direct and indirect taxes

Overall, gender budget work has tended to focus on the expenditure side of the budget rather than on revenue. The main exception is the UK, where much of the work of the Women's Budget Group has focused on tax-related measures such as the child tax credit. The Group used arguments around unpaid care work in its interaction with the British Treasury. In March 2002, the Chancellor announced that the child tax credit would, from 2003, be paid to the main caregiver. Thus, in practice it would usually be paid to the woman. The Treasury was mainly convinced by arguments of efficiency – that money paid to a woman is more likely to be used to benefit the child than money paid to a man.

Box 24: Looking at Taxation

Analysing taxation means looking at national and local taxes imposed on individuals, companies (and other organisations) and goods and services. The research should cover the following areas:

- A description of the situation of women and men, and different groups of women and men (e.g. rich and poor, people in different geographical areas), in respect of characteristics that influence both the impact of different forms of taxation (e.g. employment status, consumption patterns, etc) and the need for goods and services funded by government revenue;

- A description of taxation policy at the national and local levels, and an assessment of differences in how these might affect women and men and different groups of women and men;

- A description of the amounts collected and planned to be collected from different types of taxes in recent years and the current year;

- Estimates of how much of each of the taxes was/would be paid by women and men (and different groups of women and men).

Within developing countries, South Africa, Tanzania and Uganda have conducted some analyses of tax and local government revenue. One reason for less attention being paid to revenue in developing countries is the very small proportion of the population that pays direct taxes, as well as the very limited number of – if any – benefits delivered through the tax system. Also, the shape of revenue probably differs much more between countries than the shape of expenditure. It is thus more difficult for lessons to be learnt from experiences across the developed-developing country divide.

In terms of the distributional effects of tax regimes, direct taxes such as personal income tax tend to fall more on men because of their greater presence in the formal labour force, more senior positions and higher incomes. Additional gender biases can occur in the form of marriage penalties. For example, couples filing joint returns may incur a greater tax liability than if they filed as single individuals, or tax on the second income in a household might begin at a higher level than the base rate of tax. Gender bias can also occur when non-labour income (from assets, savings, property or business) or tax expenditures (subsidies, deductions, exemptions or credits) are allocated to the male spouse or not available to a married woman who is the sole earner.

Indirect taxes, such as value-added or consumption taxes, may appear to be gender neutral because they are attached to products and services rather than gendered people. However, these taxes tend to have a greater impact on poor people, who spend a higher percentage of their income on consumer goods and thus end up paying a larger share of their income on such taxes. Indirect taxes also have a greater impact on women, who are disproportionately represented among the poor and make proportionately higher contributions to household consumption budgets than men.

The tendency of civil society work on gender and revenue has often been to argue for the lowering of various taxes. In fact, however, gender equity might often be better promoted through an increase in direct taxes. This is because men are more likely to earn cash income, and thus more likely to contribute to taxes, while women are more likely to contribute to society through unpaid labour that does not generate income and so does not attract taxes. By levying taxes on those who benefit from cash income, government can increase the money it has available to implement, among others, programmes that reduce the burden of unpaid labour on women and girls.

Other types of government revenue

Beyond tax, user fee systems have been increasingly implemented since the 1980s as countries undergoing structural adjustment have been encouraged to introduce them for basic social services. Many governments have come to see user fees as an alternative to tax-based financing for a range of public services. Supporters of user fees argue that they increase efficiency, effectiveness and even equity. However, there is very little evidence to support these claims. On the other hand,

Indirect taxes, such as value-added or consumption taxes, may appear to be gender neutral because they are attached to products and services rather than gendered people. However, these taxes tend to have a greater impact on poor people [and] women.

The need to investigate donor funds is not simply about turning the tables. It also raises important questions about the government's own approach to budgeting.

there is some disturbing evidence of reductions in equity after the introduction of user fees For example, poor people's utilisation of services may decrease, with resultant negative effects on well-being and health.

Other revenue issues may be examined for possible gender impacts. These include corporate taxes, such as the granting of incentives to certain sectors as opposed to others; the impact of globalisation, specifically the reduction in customs and trade taxes; and the debt crisis and the fiscal drain of debt servicing.

Donor funds

One area where there has been surprisingly little gender analysis is that of donor contributions to country budgets. This is particularly surprising in countries where donors are responsible for very large proportions of government revenue. In South Africa, where donor funds account for less than 2 per cent of the government budget, there have been two analyses. The first formed part of the Fourth Women's Budget and the second was commissioned as part of the government's own development cooperation report.

In Mozambique, gender budget work within government suggested that documents relating to donor-funded projects could be a rich source of information. In Bangladesh, too, budget analysis of donor funds seems easier than of other funds, as donors are interested in promoting new systems that tell them what is happening in respect of their contributions. However, in countries such as Tanzania, donor funds are among the last aspects planned to be included in new budgeting systems. Government officials have real doubts as to whether they will get access to the information they need.

The need to investigate donor funds is not simply about turning the tables. It also raises important questions about the government's own approach to budgeting. For example, in South Africa the research revealed that a senior finance official felt that it was not necessary for government to provide much funding for the gender machinery as this area seemed to be a favourite of funders. More broadly, where donor funds form a significant proportion of the budget, how these are used and controlled relates directly to government and country ownership of their own development path.

Conclusion

This book has covered a wide range of topics, which reflects the diversity of possible avenues along which gender budget work can go. However, many areas are not covered in great depth. This is due to several factors, including the varied considerations that would arise in different countries in respect of each, the need to restrict the length of the book and the authors' own limited knowledge.

Also, initiators of GRBs do not need to consider each of the topics in depth. The intention of this guide is to give an overall sense of GRB work, and what would need to be considered depending on the path chosen. Among the most important factors determining this choice are the characteristics of the initiators (e.g. government, CSO, NGO or parliament) and the political and economic situation in the country concerned.

The first part of the guide discusses the many potential benefits of a GRB. After reading this section, readers might be left with the impression that all stakeholders will welcome a GRB. This is not the case. Budgets are about priorities and choices and thus, inevitably, there are usually losers and winners. Anyone engaging in a GRB must recognise this from the start if they are not to become despondent.

On the other hand, the guide has described how some GRBs have seen different groups working together – for example, parliamentarians and NGOs, or governments and NGOs. Initiators of GRBs would do well to think at the start about who their allies might be and to take this into consideration in planning the topics and issues to be covered.

More generally, those responsible for GRBs – especially when operating from outside government – need to think what the 'hot topics' in the national debate are. If most players are involved in a PRSP process, for example, it might be useful to make some link with that. If everyone is concerned about HIV/AIDS, that might be a good focus for the GRB work if it is to attract interest and allies. If the government is promoting programme performance budgeting and a medium-term expenditure framework, the GRB could focus on how gender aspects could be built into these developments from the start.

... promoters of gender budget work need to remember that the GRB approach is a tool and not necessarily a stand-alone exercise. The GRB message is that, unless the necessary resources are allocated, gender-sensitive policies and programmes will not succeed.

In linking up with these other issues, promoters of gender budget work need to remember that the GRB approach is a tool and not necessarily a stand-alone exercise. The GRB message is that, unless the necessary resources are allocated, gender-sensitive policies and programmes will not succeed. However, there are many other ways in which this message can be disseminated apart from a fully developed, stand-alone gender analysis of all government expenditures (see, for example, the work of the Centre for the Study of Violence and Reconciliation outlined in box 21).

Perhaps the most important final message from this guide is that undertaking a GRB is hard but rewarding work. GRBs seldom achieve instant results, and patience is usually required in order to properly understand the methodology, identify the entry points, build alliances and develop a programme. In addition, partly because it is a political process, there will be both setbacks and unexpected opportunities. However, for those who have been involved in this process it has been time well spent, and the proliferation of initiatives bears testimony to the unlimited possibilities.

Bibliography

Alexander, P. with S. Baden (2000). *Glossary on Macroeconomics from a Gender Perspective*. Report 48. BRIDGE, Institute of Development Studies, University of Sussex, Brighton.

BRIDGE (2001). 'Briefing Paper on the "Feminisation of Poverty"'. Report No 59. Prepared for the Swedish International Development Cooperation Agency. Institute of Development Studies, University of Sussex, Brighton.

—— (2002). *Cutting-Edge Pack on Gender and Budgets*. Institute of Development Studies, University of Sussex, Brighton.

Budlender, D. (1991). 'Women, Education and the Economy.' In *Proceedings of the Student Service Centre Natal Workshop: Bursaries towards a Free and Democratic Education System*. Students Service Centre, Cape Town.

—— (2000). 'The Political Economy of Women's Budgets in the South'. In *World Development* 28(7). Special Gender Issue, July.

——, D. Elson, G. Hewitt and T. Mukhopadhyay (2002). *Gender Budgets Make Cents*. Commonwealth Secretariat, London.

Budlender, D. and G. Hewitt (eds) (2002). *Gender Budgets Make More Cents*. Commonwealth Secretariat, London.

Budlender, D. and R. Sharp with K. Allen (1998). *How to Do a Gender-Sensitive Budget Analysis: Contemporary Research and Practice*. Commonwealth Secretariat/AusAID, London.

Bunker, R. (2000). 'Villages as a Positive Force for Good Governance: The right to information and India's struggle against grass-roots corruption'. In *United Nations Chronicle* (Online Edition) 38(1).

De Bruyn, J. and D. Budlender (1998). 'Intergovernmental Fiscal Relations'. In D. Budlender (ed.) *The Third Women's Budget*. Institute for Democracy in South Africa, Cape Town.

Demery, L. (1996). 'Gender and Public Social Spending: Disaggregating benefit incidence'. Unpublished paper, Poverty and Social Policy Department, World Bank, Washington DC.

Elson, D. (1997) 'Gender-Neutral, Gender-Blind, or Gender-Sensitive Budgets? Changing the Conceptual Framework to Include Women's Empowerment and the Economy of Care'. Preparatory Country Mission to Integrate Gender into National Budgetary Policies and Procedures in the Context of Economic Reform. Background paper prepared for the Commonwealth Secretariat, London.

—— (2002a). 'Annex: Gender Responsive Budget Analytical Tools'. In Budlender *et al. Gender Budgets Make Cents*. Commonwealth Secretariat, London.

—— (2002b). 'What's Behind the Budget? Politics, rights and accountability'. In A. Norton and D. Norton (eds) *The Budget Process*. Overseas Development Institute (ODI), London.

Elson, D. and N. Cagatay (1999). 'Engendering Macroeconomic Policy and Budgets for Sustainable Human Development'. Human Development Report Office, UNDP, New York.

Esim, S. (1995). 'Gender Equity Concerns in Public Expenditure: Methodologies and concerns'. Paper prepared for the World Bank Annual Meeting of the Special Program of Assistance for Africa Working Group on Poverty and Social Policy, Ottawa.

Falk, S. and I. Shapiro (1999). *A Guide to Budget Work*. International Budget Project, Centre on Budget and Policy Priorities, Washington DC.

Folscher, A., W. Krafchik and I. Shapiro (2001). *Transparency and Participation in the Budget Process: South Africa Country Report*. Institute for Democracy in South Africa, Cape Town.

Foster, M. and A. Fozzard (2000). *Aid and Public Expenditure: A Guide*. Overseas Development Institute (ODI), London.

Fundar and Equidad de Genero (1999). 'Women Leaders Getting In: Advocacy skills building for gender-sensitive public speaking'. San Angel, Mexico.

Goetz, A.M. (1994). 'From Feminist Knowledge to Data for Development: The bureaucratic management of information on women and development'. In *IDS Bulletin* 25(2):27–36.

Govender, Pregs (1996). 'Foreword'. In D. Budlender (ed.) *The Women's Budget*. Institute for Democracy in South Africa, Cape Town.

Healey, J. and W. Tordoff (eds) (1995). *Votes and Budgets: Comparative Studies in Accountable Governance in the South*. St. Martin's Press, New York.

Hedman, B., F. Perucci and P. Sundström (1996). *Engendering Statistics: A Tool for Change*. Statistics Sweden, Stockholm.

Holmes, M. (1998). *Public Expenditure Management Handbook* (draft). Poverty Reduction and Economic Management, World Bank, Washington DC.

International Budget Project, The (2000). 'A Taste of Success: Examples of the budget work of NGOs'. Center on Budget and Policy Priorities, Washington, DC, October.

Inter-Parliamentary Union (2001). 'Parliament and the Budget

Process including from a Gender Perspective'. Report No. 38. IPU, Geneva.

Klugman, J. (ed.) (2002). *A Sourcebook for Poverty Reduction Strategies*. World Bank, Washington DC.

Krafchik, W. (2002). 'Can Civil Society Add Value to Budget Decision-Making?' In *Gender Budget Initiatives: Strategies, Concepts and Experiences*. Papers from a High Level International Conference 'Strengthening Economic and Financial Governance Through Gender Responsive Budgeting', Brussels, 16–17 October 2001. UNIFEM, New York.

Narayan, D. (ed.) (2002). *Empowerment and Poverty Reduction: A Sourcebook*. World Bank, Washington DC.

Organisation for Economic Cooperation and Development (2001). *The DAC Guidelines on Poverty Reduction*. OECD, Paris.

Pradhan, S. (1996). *Evaluating Public Spending: A Framework for Public Expenditure Reviews*. Discussion Paper 323, World Bank, Washington DC.

Sarraf, F. (2003). 'Gender-Responsive Government Budgeting'. IMF Working Paper WP03/83. Fiscal Affairs Department, International Monetary Fund, Washington, DC.

Schiavo-Campo, S. and D. Tommasi (1999). *Managing Government Expenditure*. Asian Development Bank, Philippines.

Scholz, W., M. Cichon and K. Hagemejer (1999). *Social Budgeting*. International Labour Organization, Geneva.

Sen, G. (1999). *Gender Mainstreaming in Finance*. Commonwealth Secretariat, London.

Shapiro, I. (ed.) (2001). *A Guide to Budget Work for NGOs*. International Budget Project, Center on Budget and Policy Priorities, Washington DC.

Songco, D. (undated). 'Accountability to the Poor: Experiences in civic engagement in public expenditure management' (draft report). Participation Group and Social Development Department, World Bank, Washington DC.

Stark, A. and S. de Vylder (1998). *Mainstreaming Gender in Namibia's National Budget*. Swedish International Development Cooperation Agency, Stockholm.

Taylor, V. (1999). *Gender Mainstreaming in Development Planning*. Commonwealth Secretariat, London.

United Nations (2000). *The World's Women 2000: Trends and Statistics*. United Nations, New York.

United Nations Development Fund for Women (UNIFEM) (2002). *Gender Budget Initiatives: Strategies, Concepts and Experiences*. UNIFEM, New York.

United Nations Development Programme (1995). *Human Development Report*. UNDP, New York.

—— (2002). Human Development Report. United Nations Development Programme, New York.

van de Walle, D. (1998). 'Assessing the Welfare Impacts of Public Spending'. In *World Development* 26(3).

World Bank (2001). *Engendering Development: Through Gender Equality in Rights, Resources, and Voice*. World Bank Policy Research Report. Oxford University Press, Washington DC.

—— (2002). 'Integrating Gender into the World Bank: A strategy for action'. World Bank, Washington DC.